"DON'T TELL JUDY 'NO'!"

JUDITH ANN LOREDO Ph.D.
and ALEX MONTOYA

Author's Tranquility Press
MARIETTA, GEORGIA

Judith Ann Loredo/Author's Tranquility Press
2706 Station Club Drive SW
Marietta, GA 30060
www.authorstranquilitypress.com

Ordering Information:
Quantity sales. Special discounts are available on quantity purchases by corporations, associations, and others. For details, contact the "Special Sales Department" at the address above.

"Don't Tell Judy 'No'!"/Judith Ann Loredo
Paperback: 978-1-959453-45-1
eBook: 978-1-959453-46-8

Dedication

I dedicate this book first and foremost to my creator who led me down this journey of life—I am eternally grateful for his guidance and faith strong life he lead me to follow!

I dedicate this book to my life's inspirations:
my parents, Judge Jaime and Juliette Gutierrez;
my aunt Victoria Ramos; ;
my beloved husband, Eleuterio "Sonny" Loredo;
my children, Alysa Denise Lozano Muto and Lloyd Eleuterio Loredo;
my grandchildren, Alessia Juliette Muto and Demetre Dominic Muto;
my lifelong friends, who are like my sisters;
my students, who have allowed me to serve as their professor and mentor;
my mentors, who guided me throughout my career in K−12 education and higher education;
my dear friend and former administrative assistant who transcribed and typed this entire book, Mary Comerford;
and to all who walk this way but once, and want to make a difference, or their passing will have been in vain.

My Bridget Cleary Karam Photographer for the beautiful picture for the cover of my book...you were there when I needed your help!

Contents

Introduction

Making a Difference

People have always told me, "Judy, your life is a journey, and it has been a remarkable one. You should write a book!"

Honestly, I have been too busy dedicating myself to helping as many students as I can to get an education. I believe that my life story is worth telling, but when would I have time to tell it? Even more importantly, how would I write it when I have always been challenged by putting my thoughts on paper? Because of my father's tutelage, my greatest strength since I was a young girl was articulating my thoughts through my speaking ability. I shied away from writing as much as possible, and I have always used the medium of speech to convey my thoughts.

Well, in 2018, I met motivational speaker Alex Montoya when he spoke in Austin. My husband, Sonny, and I hosted a reception for him at our house. At dinner that night, as we exchanged life stories, he told me, "Judy, you should write a book ... and I'll help you!" That was enough for me to believe in divine intervention. And in the need to tell this story so that others, especially students, might believe in themselves in spite of any learning deficiencies they might experience.

That's what this book is all about: my family and my personal history in overcoming obstacles, achieving beyond anyone's expectation, and serving others. I want people to know that no matter what others may tell you, you *can* succeed, and whatever you set out to do, you can make a difference!

There are countless people to acknowledge and to thank for who I have become. If I have accidently omitted anyone, please charge that to my head and not my heart. I would be remiss if I did not thank the following individuals for both their tangible and intangible, direct and indirect, advice and support along my life's journey in education.

First and foremost, I thank Almighty God and Mother Mary for my faith and resilience. I thank my life inspirations, my parents, grandparents, aunts, and uncles who raised me. I am especially grateful to the following individuals: Mary Margaret and Mike Bias, who were like second parents to me after I lost my own; Ginger DeLeon Sutton, Elizabeth Villeagas, Lillie Delgado, Elida Vasquez, Carol Garcia, Wayde Frey, and Mary Comerford, who served as my administrative and worked tirelessly to help me succeed in my role as an educator; the Southside ISD Board of Trustees that hired me as their superintendent and changed my life forever, Irene Martinez, and Larry Rourke;

Dr. Gregory Vincent; Dr. Ben Harris; Dr. Jim Yates; Dr. Otilia Vidaurri; Dr. David Jimenez; Dr. Bill Kirby; Dr. Tom Anderson; Dr. Nolan Estes; Dr. John Q. Taylor King; Dr. Joe McMillan; Dr. Larry Ervin; Dr. Lenora Waters; Dr. Sandra Vaughan; Dr. Jennifer Davies; Margarete Norris; Dr. Alicia Moore; Dr. Eric Budd; Dr. Raymond Paredes; Dr. David Gardner; Linda Battles; the faculty and staff at Huston- Tillotson University, especially Dr. Rosalee Martin and Dr. Michel Hirsch; and the staff and administrators of the Texas Higher Education Coordinating

Board, especially Susan Brown, Dr. McGregor Stevenson, Dr. Vann Davis, Dr. Garry Tomerlin, and Dr. Kristen Kramer. The advice and support that all those listed here afforded to me throughout my educational career has not gone unnoticed, and I remain eternally grateful because each played a part in the person that I have become.

A very special thank-you to my beloved husband, Sonny, who, when he asked me to marry him, said he wanted me to stay at home and be a wife and mother to my daughter because he was raised with the belief that the husband was to be the provider for the household. In spite of that request, he agreed to my returning to work after a few years of marriage, and throughout the past thirty-seven years, he has supported me faithfully and showered me with love through every endeavor I have undertaken in my educational pursuits.

Sonny and I were married on a beautiful sunny Saturday afternoon on May 7, 1983. He had four daughters, and I had a daughter. We became a blended family, and then on October 14, 1988, our son, Lloyd Eleuterio, was born.

A profound thank-you goes out to my daughter, Alysa Denise. I extend that to her because throughout her childhood and growing-up years, there were many times I could not be present for special events due to job commitments. Yet she always had a smile on her face and was proud of every accomplishment that came my way.

To my son, Lloyd, I thank you for always being there for me but most importantly, for taking my advice as you walked your own journey of life and education. To my stepdaughters, Virginia, Dolores, Veronica, and Delisa, I thank you for the joys you've brought to my life, and I hope that in some way, I have had a positive impact on yours. Thanks to all our children, we are blessed with five sons-in-law, one daughter-in-law, twenty-one grandchildren, and nine great-grandchildren.

We are very proud that one of our grandsons, who is a brother with the Order of the Brothers and Sisters of Charity and all our children and older grandchildren have completed their formal education. Some have already completed master's degrees, and others are presently in pursuit of their own advanced degrees as well.

Really, my life has been all about those students who have given me the opportunity to touch their lives. It has been spent fighting for my own education, striving to ensure others receive theirs, and remaining committed to improving public and higher education and increasing access for all. Believing I have made a difference in the lives of the students I taught, I live by this saying: "I shall walk this way but once. And I shall make a difference, or my passing will have been in vain."

I do hope you enjoy reading about my life's journey. Hopefully, you'll see your life story within mine. Please know you can do anything you set out to achieve as long as you believe in yourself and as long as you stay true to yourself.

CHAPTER 1

Family Roots

Duty Calls

My father, Jaime Pedraja Gutierrez, was born near the turn of the last century in Torreon, Mexico. He lived there until he was thirteen years old. As the second oldest of eight brothers, he quickly learned the meaning of discipline and responsibility.

When you are in the upper tier of a group of siblings, you're expected to help take care of them. That was one of the lessons taught by Jaime's parents, who lived a simple life and then decided to migrate to the United States. They chose as their new home the shining jewel of Texas—San Antonio.

Jaime's responsibilities quickly changed from elder-brother duties. He was now expected to work in order to help support the entire clan. Balancing work and studies at Brackenridge High School proved difficult, and before long, Jaime dropped out of school. Besides, any student needs to be furnished with clothes, supplies, and money for activities. His parents deemed all of that as less important than helping the family make ends meet. So Jaime bade farewell to schooling. Many of his friends considered this to be a shameful waste of a brilliant mind. Jaime was a very articulate individual. He was ultra-aware of the world around him. Like most immigrants, he carried the sobering memories of moving to a new country and all the challenges, fears, and hopes that come with traversing a new land.

He spoke both English and *Español*, which by itself was not particularly unique. The fact that he communicated in both languages without an accent, however, was. Those around him noted that he spoke in both tongues not just plainly but beautifully. Whether he was at home, school (while he was still there), or at work, his smooth, almost lyrical command of the languages shone through. It was not simply saved for one situation or place solely. But work responsibilities did beckon, so as a young man, Jaime did odd jobs. He sold newspapers, shined shoes, and did whatever he could do to help his mother and father, and younger siblings survive.

At a young age, Jaime realized that he had an ear for music. One day he had the pleasure and fortune of meeting the owner of the Alamo Piano Music Company, Alfred Flores Sr. His store was located on Main Avenue in San Antonio. They sold gorgeous pianos throughout the gorgeous city. As proof of his great intelligence and resolve, Jaime never took piano lessons yet still taught himself how to tickle the ivories. He had never taken piano lessons but had a natural ear for music. So he took the very unorthodox route of teaching himself how to play piano. This got him hired by Mr. Flores. Jaime proved he could personally show Alamo Piano Music Company's customers the quality of the musical instrument he was attempting to sell them. Hearing sweet and gorgeous music directly played on the piano—from a self-taught, erstwhile pianist no less—could result in them purchasing one.

In 1932, another beautiful figure wafted into Jaime's life—a fresh-faced, dark-haired, fair-skinned stunning young lady named Maria Juliette Ramos. He was struck by her right away, and as forthrightly as he learned how to play and sell pianos, he asked her out. She said yes.

Juliette, of course, is my mother. She was born, as Marty Robbins once crooned, "out in the West Texas town of El Paso." The hardscrabble town of El Paso, which borders Mexico, was her first home. There she resided as the oldest child of Manuel and Maria Ramos. Juliette had three other siblings—two younger brothers, David and Manuel, and my dear Aunt Vickie, who would be like a second mother to me throughout my childhood.

At a young age, Juliette and her family moved to San Antonio. My grandmother, Maria, worked as a seamstress, so I was always dressed in beautiful, frilly lace dresses. Juliette, as a teenager, worked at Kress Department Store for many years. She graduated from Fox Tech High School and then went to work for the Child Support Office of Bexar County.

Now Jaime's courtship of her was no fly-by-night endeavor. It was like a melodic piano ensemble—long and slow and enduringly romantic. They dated for eight years, right in the throes of the Great Depression. As much as she enjoyed the courtship, Juliette admitted to friends that if it had not been for the war, she probably would never have gotten married to Jaime. It just took him so darn long! But in 1940, they did marry. Both Jaime and Juliette were by then in their late twenties. Of course, a year later, disaster struck America. An ambush attack by Japanese forces was unleashed on the Hawaiian island of Pearl Harbor. December 7, 1941, was regarded by President Roosevelt as a "date which will live in infamy." Suddenly, the United States was involved in World War II.

Jaime, still relatively a newlywed, was called to serve his country. He went on to serve six years in the United States Army. His primary stationing was in Hawaii, where he served under the legendary General Nimitz. Nimitz now has a carrier ship named after him. Again displaying his tireless work ethic that served him so well as a self-taught pianist and piano salesman, Jaime rose to the rank of chief warrant officer. When World War II ended, he returned to San Antonio. Juliette joyfully welcomed him home. He was a hero and a husband all at once. Like so many baby boomer couples of that era, the Gutierrezes were eager to start a family and live in peacetime.

Jaime had another interest as well. He was quite engaged in politics. This led him to search for ways he could seek out volunteer opportunities to serve those less fortunate within the Latino community. His dream was to become an attorney. But although the desire was there, the necessary finances were not. So he compromised, telling Juliette he would hold off on returning to school until a few years later. Thus, Jaime returned to selling pianos. He did that masterfully enough that he also took on selling cars. The strong work ethic again shone through in both jobs, and he saved and saved until he could go to school.

But just as his sales roles were growing, another change came: one of Jaime's brothers owned a mortuary in sunny California. So his brother, Raymond, invited him to head west and learn that business. The mortuary was located on Broadway in downtown Los Angeles, quite close to Chinatown.

So my father put his schooling dreams aside and moved by himself to the Golden State. Under my Uncle Raymond's tutelage, he spent several years there, learning the mortuary business.

But mother knew that his dream was to be an attorney and enter into politics. So when I was four years old, she sent my grandmother and me to California to bring my dad back home. It was a critical time for my family because my mother said she did not want to live on the second floor above a mortuary and raise a child. She gave my father an offer and ultimatum: he could come back to San Antonio and apply to St. Mary's University and go back to school and realize his dream of becoming a lawyer. She was willing to work and support our family so that he could realize his dream. Really, this was the first true adversity in my parents' married life. My mother, in her heart, knew that she could not live above a mortuary. It made no sense to her to live in such a vibrant and happy place as California and be surrounded by the morbidity of death. So she challenged my father to return to San Antonio. She felt he had enough of undertakers. It was time for him to undertake the study of law, which had always been his dream. He was not surprised but was still touched that she was willing to support the family so he could achieve this longtime dream. So my father agreed to it.

He moved back to San Antonio and petitioned St. Mary's University for admission. The university told him he would immediately be considered a probationary student. Dropping out of high school to assist his parents and siblings meant there were still incomplete requirements to fulfill. Papa agreed to those terms and displayed his usual determination and tenacity. During the day, he was in class at St. Mary's University. At night, he sold used automobiles on Broadway. He was always extremely supportive of family needs financially and emotionally. He was a fantastic dad. After much toiling and grinding, he earned his doctorate of jurisprudence. Not only that, he graduated from St. Mary's with honors!

My father hadn't returned to school until well into his early forties because money for education was tight. Even though he used his GI Bill in order to get educated, we still needed to live. My mother was a high school graduate, but she was a clerk in the Child Support Office, although her salary was not high. But he never gave up on his dreams. His career was a fast journey, and he thrived on becoming involved in San Antonio political scene. Upon graduation from law school, he joined the District Attorney's Office as chief of domestic relations. After a few years of experience under his belt, he decided to open up a private law practice on the twenty-sixth floor of the Tower Life Building. His private practice days led him to his first judgeship when the commissioners' court appointed him a municipal court judge. After several years in that position, the commissioner court tapped him to becoming one of the main JP Judges, a position he held for twenty-six years. Judge Jimmie, as he was called, was loved and respected by the Hispanic community of San Antonio. He was known as the marrying judge because of the number of couples he had married throughout his judgeship. He was an extremely articulate individual who was fluent in both English and Spanish. He was called upon frequently to serve as master of ceremonies for many events in the Hispanic community.

I firmly believe that watching my father pursue his dreams; taking his advice that no matter what you set out to do in life, always be the best that you can be at whatever you do; and learning from him how to approach a podium and sound intelligent has provided me motivation as a student, educator, and passionate philanthropist!

A Glorious Time

My grandparents on my mother's side were especially devout Catholics. This was due in part to Juliette having an aunt on her father's side who was a nun in the Sisters of Loretto, dear Sister Manuelita. Every year my mother would be sent to study at Loretto Academy in Santa Fe, New Mexico. She did that throughout her childhood until she entered high school. That's when she returned to San Antonio to attend Fox Tech High School. She was a bright girl, but her family was poor. They just did not have the means to send her to college after graduation. So she went to work. For many years, she toiled at Kress Five and Dime Store.

Soon after graduation from high school, Juliette met that charming tall, dark-haired, green-eyed Jaime P. Gutierrez. My mother met this charming gentleman who could dance and walk with confidence at a dance sponsored by the Selene Club, a young ladies' organization founded by Mrs. Magnon, a well-known and respected lady in the Hispanic community. Juliette's parents took her to the dances, for you see, in those days, dating was not as we think of it today. Parents were chaperones without question. Jaime and Juliette would become friends and start dating, but it would be ten years from the day they met before they would marry. My mother used to say that if it had not been for World War II when my father was called to serve in the army (achieving the rank of chief warrant officer in the army assigned to General Nimitz's staff), she might never have gotten married. My parents were married on April 12, 1940, in San Antonio, Texas, at Little Flower Catholic Church. My father left to serve his country, and my mother remained in San Antonio, living with her mother (my grandma Ramos) and my aunt Vickie at 507 Jackson St. After the war ended, my dad returned home to continue his life with my mother. Then I was born in early autumn—October 10, 1946. My family was extremely loving and devoted their entire lives to helping me develop, grow, and mature into a fine young woman. The old saying "It takes a village to raise a child" was proven in our family. Helping to raise me were my grandmother and Aunt Vickie, both of whom doted on me endlessly. With my father and mother both relentlessly working, my *Abuela*, Grandma Ramos, cared for me during the day. Then after the hot sun disappeared into the cool Texas night, Abuela, Auntie, and Mom took care of me in the evenings. My dad jokingly said I made up for the ten children they *didn't* have! We really did not have much, but as a child, I did not know that. Childhood seemed normal and fun. We went everywhere by city bus because we did not own a car until I was seven.

The following year, we got our first television. Oh, it was a glorious time! As a *familia*, we listened to everything on the radio and on balmy evenings; we would chatter on the house porch or walk throughout our neighborhood. In those days, of course, the crime rate was so low that we didn't give a second thought about walking outside, playing outdoors, or even sleeping with the windows open. My grandmother worked as a seamstress, and she made all my clothes. I was always dressed in frills and lace and was never allowed to wear pants. God forbid that I would ever play in dirt; I was taught very early that I was a girl, and girls should always be nicely dressed with hair well-groomed. Without question, this philosophy had a lasting impact on me throughout my life. But a dark point did come when my grandmother became ill. By then, my parents and aunt were working, so I was placed in St. Anthony's daycare. It was directly across the street from where my mother and father worked in the San Antonio courthouse. My mother would drop me off in the morning and then confidently stride to her office. When I was five, she took me to Ursuline Academy. It was time to be enrolled in the first grade.

Mischievous and Precocious

At that time, you did not have to be enrolled as a six-year-old by September 1. I was accepted, which made my parents happy, but I did not like it there, which made them decidedly unhappy.

I did not enjoy school at all! Both the nuns and school buildings were old and creepy, in my opinion. Being mischievous and precocious, I was determined to get expelled. I really didn't know what that meant, but common sense told me if I acted badly enough, the nuns would ask me to leave. We had these old desks with lids the students could lift up to put their books inside. So one day, I lifted up my lid, put my sweater around my head, and slipped my head under the desk. Then I stuffed the arms of my sweater with paper and proudly lifted my head up so that the sister would notice me. I resembled an airplane ready to take off.

The kids around me chuckled, but I remained silent. Then I stood up so that Sister could really see me because she had not noticed me looking like Air Judy. I figured that by standing up, I would catch her eye. She saw me all right, with the admonition, "Judith Ann, please come to the front of the room immediately."

Stubbornly, I trudged to the front of the classroom with my sweater still tied around my head. My classmates were outright giggling now.

"Young lady," Sister said sternly, "sit at the bottom of my desk!"

Her desk was on a raised platform because that was the only way she and the other old nuns could see and keep up with us first graders. So I obliged. And I was quiet.

And I got bored.

With her feet on the platform right beside me, at eye level, the opportunity was too good to resist. As she droned on about something or other to the class, I gently reached for her shoes.

And tied her shoelaces together.

The next sound I heard was *wham*!

She fell—she wasn't hurt—and the room was filled with the cackles of kids laughing uproariously.

From there, I was sent to the cloakroom as punishment. But the isolation allowed me to tie all the arms of student sweaters and jackets together. Surely I'd be expelled now, right? I expected my parents to get a phone call saying I was not allowed to come back. I was wrong. The nuns always found a way to keep us, even the misbehaving youngsters. I think it's because they needed the tuition money.

Discouraged but not drastically deterred, I knew tomorrow was another day. A new opportunity to think, plot, and plan a better way to actually get expelled. The Texas sun rose and with it, so did my deviousness. This time, I would get on the playground swing set and swing hard and free. I swung as rapidly and as high as I could. My hope was that I would fall off. If I did, I'd probably get hurt.

And if I was hurt and injured, surely the nuns would be forced to send me home!

Well, I suppose the only thing greater than my fearlessness or recklessness was my natural athletic ability. I didn't fall. My butt remained firmly planted on that swing no matter how high I went!

Still, I was determined. So I allowed the swing to ease into a gradual slowdown and jumped off. I resembled a high jumper landing both feet into the gravelly skybox, although that was far more graceful than I had been hoping for. If I wasn't a good trickster, perhaps I could be an effective actress. As if a hundred onions were sliced right in front of me, on command, I started crying. The nuns were perplexed at my sudden stream of tears and sobbing, so I was half-right—they allowed me to call home.

My mother answered the phone and deciphered my tearful tale.

"Mama," I said, sobbing, "I broke my nose." Calmly she replied, "Is it bleeding?"

"No."

"Is it swollen?" "No."

She sighed, but I maintained my ruse of remaining upset. So she left our house, drove to Ursuline Academy, and picked me up. I knew that was only a temporary reprieve, so I decided to inject some honesty into my shenanigans. That night, I stood before both my parents. And I told them quite sincerely that I strongly disliked

Ursuline. I was truly afraid being there because the school was old, and the nuns were old, and both were quite scary. I prepared for the inevitable pushback of my objections. And probably a lecture on the need to just calm down and focus on my studies. But those two things never came. Instead, what my parents offered was empathy, understanding, and the reasoning that I couldn't focus on my various subjects if I hated a place.

Mom and Dad looked at each other and excused themselves momentarily. When they returned, my father looked directly into my eyes and said, "Mija, we want you to be happy, safe, and eager to learn. Tomorrow, we will take you downtown and enroll you at St. Mary's Catholic School."

I was elated! I was saddened, though, because it meant leaving my dear friend, Geri Greenleaf. Since I was about four years old, we had been best of friends. But I also realized our friendship would indeed continue even though we were in different schools. Our mothers, after all, were like sisters.

CHAPTER 2

Divine Providence

I Will Not Let You Fail

From the day I transferred to St. Mary's Catholic School as a first grader, I was happy. I loved that place. Many wonderful memories flood my mind instantly: attending Mass every day, learning the language and meaning of the Latin Mass, and though they were sad occasions, singing songs in Latin at funerals held at St. Mary's Cathedral Church. Part of our weekly tradition and instruction was to be in Sunday Mass by nine o'clock in the morning. This was required of all students. But it never felt like a chore or drag. St. Mary's was just so vibrant and beautiful.

After Mass, the students would skip and run to the doughnut shop across the street for delicious doughnuts. It was spirituality and camaraderie all in one. I treasure those memories. Aside from loving the doughnuts and Coney Island, a wonderful hangout for hot dogs, I made close friends.

One of the first girls I met was Sonia Conle, who became my mother's godchild. Sonia's mother wanted her baptized, but her parents did not know anyone who could fulfill the baptism role as godparents. So the pastor at St. Mary's asked my mother and father if they would serve as Sonia's godparents. They agreed, and our friendship became strong as a Texas oak tree. There was also Patsy Turner and Elida Gonzalez and Carol Trejo. They became my treasured friends, with Elida really becoming my bestie. Even as a young girl, I remember telling Sonia, Patsy, Carol and Elida, "I love you girls. We're going to be friends forever." And I meant it.

My first two years there went very smoothly. I felt no need to display my mischievous or precocious side. I was engaged in learning and happily so. But third grade proved to be tougher. I hit a proverbial brick wall. You see, even though I was learning, it was primarily through memory. The nuns did not realize I really could not read. It was not until the end of my third grade that they discovered I was not reading at a third-grade level. This prompted a meeting with my parents. The nuns informed them I would not be passed through to fourth grade. My parents were, of course, very upset.

My mother turned to me and said, "I will teach you how to read." Then she added, "I will not let you fail!"

So that summer, I spent each and every day in the public library. My mother accompanied me and taught me to read every children's book she could get her hands on. I read and I read and I read.

Finally, at the end of summer, I was tested. I just barely passed. But I did pass, and I was allowed to move on to fourth grade.

This is where a vicious cycle began. Although I could read every word in a book, it was because I had become an excellent sight reader. I did not remember anything I had read, nor could I comprehend enough to explain it. But I believe the sisters did not care because their only concern was that I read well. So whenever I was called upon in class to read, I did so perfectly. As a result, my English grades were flawless. But it was also in fourth grade that I realized I did not excel in math either. I liked arithmetic very much but truly could not understand the concepts.

Can you imagine? I was an excellent reader that had no retention, was not a good writer, and also struggled with math. What a mess! And frankly, that set the stage for the rest of my school years. I continued to work hard year after year. By the time I was a teenager, I also developed a love for volleyball. *Who knows*, I thought, *maybe someday I could be famous as a volleyball player.* But my mother had different intentions. She wanted me to be a concert pianist. She had taken piano lessons for eighteen years, and Daddy had taught himself the piano, and both could play absolutely beautifully. So I earnestly tried but to no avail. It became painfully evident I had not inherited that musical gene or could learn through grueling lessons. I was grateful she did allow me to play volleyball. But Mother also reminded me that when I grew up and went to a party, all I would be able to do was "volley a ball" because I would not know what to do in front of a piano. This lowered my confidence, as did struggling in classes and succeeding only in earning grades just high enough to pass. Also lowering my confidence was the fact that whenever I tried out for something—like the school volleyball team—I was only able to make the B team. Not only was the A team seemingly more athletic, those kids got selected for important campus leadership roles too. We didn't, and I didn't.

That low confidence resulted in me not having any interest in trying to be a school leader, like running for student office or participating in any extracurricular activities. Part of that was my family's limited financial resources but also just not believing I was worthy of attempting these things. I just felt, overall, I was not good enough.

Second to Nun

Still, I did love St. Mary's. I graduated and then had to decide where to attend high school.

But just as I began this process, it made me realized I may want to become a nun. After all, I was always with the sisters, and they seemingly enjoyed their life. And I enjoyed being around them.

So at age fourteen, just one year into being a teen, I entered the novitiate of the Sisters of Divine Providence located at the motherhouse in tiny Castroville, Texas. My parents, especially my mother, were delighted.

When I saw that the nuns there slept on small cots, rose at dawn, and spent time exclusively in prayer in the mornings before being allowed to communicate in the afternoon, I was shocked. This was not what I saw the sisters do on my school campus! We also had daily chores, which I didn't mind, because I had responsibilities at home too. Still, it did not take long to see that being a nun was not the life for me. After just one week of unhappiness and homesickness that descended upon me like the heavy summer humidity, I called my parents to ask them to pick me up. I wanted to go home. This declaration shattered my mother's dreams. She had been thrilled that I wanted to be a nun because that could be her direct pipeline to God. Now that pipeline was instantly bursting.

On My Own Two Feet

Now the 1960s were upon us. A brand new decade of promise and hope, with our nation's first Catholic president in John F. Kennedy. Under this canopy and context of excitement, I started looking at where I wanted to go to high school. I knew I did not want to return to Ursuline. There was also the University of the Incarnate Word, which was basically a school for the rich. Also, St. Francis and St. Gerard, but both of them were too far from where I lived. There was also Providence High School, which was fairly close to home and both of my parents' workplaces. I had started my education with the Sisters of Divine Providence and had already completed my education from first grade through eighth grade. Plus, they were right across the street from Central Catholic High, which was an all-boys school. Considering all these factors, why would I go anywhere else?

So I began my high school career at Providence High School. The boys across the street at Central Catholic wasted no time in making me feel appreciated. The immediate attention and the fact that boys were noticing me made me feel like I was really big stuff! I stayed level-headed, though, and really, my main two occupiers of time were schoolwork and playing volleyball. When I turned fifteen, I became cognizant of how much my parents were sacrificing on my behalf. So I decided that I also needed to get a job. After all, they were doing all they could to provide me with private school education. It only seemed right that I helped out.

Now by no means was Providence an Ivy League institution. It was really only a small school run by the nuns. I believe tuition was ten dollars per month, which back then was pretty substantial. But my mother felt very strongly that a Catholic environment would protect me. She did not want to worry about boys being around me all day as they were on a public school campus.

I pursued a collegiate track program because Mother wanted to be sure I would go to college. She wanted me to have the opportunities she was never given.

For so many years, she worked for the Bexar County Child Support Office. One day she told me how disheartening it was to see the local women come in on Fridays and ask for their child support checks. At times my mother would have to respond, "I'm sorry. There is no check today."

Right then and there, it became her mission to see that I was educated and could stand on my own two proverbial feet. She made it clear I should never depend on anyone to take care of me. I was instructed to provide for myself no matter the circumstances.

She often told me, "I don't want you to ever find yourself in a relationship or marriage where you cannot leave if things go wrong. You should always be able to say to someone, 'There is the door, and don't let it hit you on the way out.'"

My father was equally supportive of my schooling. Both did whatever they could to help me, so I, in turn, wanted to help out too.

At age fifteen, I commenced working at Franklin's Department Store in downtown San Antonio. I sold clothes. This gave me some spending money for fun things, so my parents couldfocus their support exclusively on my education. I didn't want to trouble them for more. I also slowly worked on my confidence and thought the best way to do this was to try out for a part in a school play. I sang in the Marian Choristers Choir and discovered that I really loved singing. (In fact, as a young girl, I would sit on the swing set in our backyard and sing like a bird—chirping away for hours.)

On Saturdays evenings, I enjoyed listening to Lawrence Welk and the big bands on the radio. That was rather odd for a teenager, but I suppose you can say I had an old soul. I enjoyed plenty of girlish fun, too, like attending school dances, rooting at the football games, and enjoying life's simple delights. It was during my time at Providence that I would meet the young man whom I would subsequently marry, David Geral Lozano. David attended Central Catholic High School and was a member of the Chaminade Guard. We dated through high school.

Now even though I was on the collegiate track, I encountered some hurtful adversity. I opted to also take courses like typing and homemaking. One day in homemaking class, Patsy Turner and I were left to clean the kitchen, which would not give us enough time to reach our next class. So we decided to put the dishes in the dishwasher and add liquid soap. We weren't trying to be mischievous; we honestly just wanted to be able to get to our next class. About two hours later, a stern voice came over the school intercom. It was the principal, Sister Maureen, who said, "Judy Gutierrez and Patsy Turner, please report to my office right now." Of course, all our classmates intoned in unison, "*Ooooooooh!*"

Patsy and I looked at each other, simultaneously gulped, and braced ourselves. We exited toward Sister Maureen's office, where she sat with Sister Agnes, our home economics teacher.

Sister Agnes spoke first, asking, "Who made the decision to place the dishes in the dishwasher?"

Meekly, I raised my hand and responded, "I did, Sister."

She then said, "Well, it's good that you're brave enough to admit it. But I'm sending you both back to the classroom to clean up the mess you created!"

Indeed, when we got back to her classroom, we discovered a room full of bubbles. No one had told us that you do not use liquid soap in a dishwasher. Or that, instead, you use special dishwasher soap. What a wet, soapy mess.

We survived that, but then a different type of adversity came in the last semester of senior year. I was taking chemistry, and because I was not good at math, I saw that becoming a chemist was definitely not in my future. So I dropped that course in favor of a second typing class. After all, shouldn't I start preparing for all the papers I'd need to type in college?

But my chemistry teacher, Sister Reparata, was highly displeased with that decision. Cornering me in the hallway, she demanded an explanation. I said, "Honestly, Sister, I just don't feel like I can succeed in that class. And I just don't want to ruin my transcript for college."

Incredulously, she looked at me square in the eyes and replied, "College? Judith Ann, if you even make it to college, I don't know if you can make it all the way through! You'll probably have to pay *them* for the degree!"

I felt humiliated. The confidence I had worked so hard to elevate instantly plummeted, but I was going to make sure what she said did not define my future.

Graduation Time

In May 1964, however, I graduated. My class had 121 girls, and I finished with a ranking of twenty-fifth. I thought about colleges, and my parents declared that if I chose a school out of town, my grandmother would have to go with me. That made me look at Our Lady of the Lake University because I was not going off to college with any grandmother!

In preparation for college, I decided to take the ACT because I thought it was easier than the SAT. Having no mentor to advise me, I did not realize the ACT was content-driven and infinitely more difficult. At Providence High I was consistently earning As in English simply because I could read. But unfortunately, I was still not retaining what I read. So when I took the ACT, I could not draw upon any background knowledge, and I struggled mightily. My score of 14 would not have gotten me into any school of choice.

Our Lady of the Lake University, also run by the Sisters of Divine Providence, offered to accept me on probation. Although that had worked out for my father, I simply disliked the idea of entering a university already being "on probation."

So I asked my parents about San Antonio Junior College. I liked that no probationary nonsense would be needed. I liked that boys and girls went to classes there in a coeducation environment. And we lived right across from campus, which negated any sort of driving or traveling expenses. Going there was simply logical. Also, tuition at Our Lady of the Lake was $25 per college hour (credit), and San Antonio Junior College was a fraction of that. My parents agreed with my rationale. I had survived high school—and Sister Reparata's doubts—and was headed to the junior college system.

In the fall semester of my freshman year, my high school boyfriend, David Lozano, decided to join the Air Force, and we got engaged. My mother was very upset because she knew for sure I would never graduate from college. My father had suffered a major heart attack and was convalescing at home for almost a year. She felt for sure I would kill him if he knew I was engaged. I knew that my dad would not be angry, so I showed him my ring, and he let me know he had seen bigger, but that he gave me his blessing. The engagement only lasted about six months because we both realized we were too young. David finished his military commitment, and we both pursued our education, not marrying till we both graduated.

CHAPTER 3

Embracing Opportunity

Learning with Limitations

I enrolled at San Antonio Junior College and formally began my college career. From the outset, I took things to an even higher level than I did in high school. I thoroughly enjoyed the classes, made many friends, and even was involved in a sorority. My immediate objective was to take the basic classes required for an associate's degree. Then I could ultimately transfer to Our Lady of the Lake University with a certificate of completion firmly in hand.

Now in the mid-1960s, things were different from today. For example, we did have admissions counselors to walk us through the process of registration. But we did not have true counselors who advised us on our strengths and weaknesses based on our high school transcripts.

Before starting my college career in 1964, I decided in the summer I would take Introduction to Psychology. I figured that because I was keenly interested in psychology, I could easily ace an intro course. How great it would be to enter San Antonio Junior College for fall semester with an A already under my belt!

To my surprise and disappointment, I did not make an A. In fact, I barely squeaked out a B.

It turned out that Intro to Psychology was an intense reading course. I found myself reading the material over and over to even remember and comprehend what I had read. This showed me the vast difference between high school and college. It also illustrated that I was still struggling with full reading comprehension. But I made it through and was ready to embark on the full schedule. I still recall my first courses: English I, Biology, History, Government, and Physical Education.

Freshman English I is still embedded in my mind. Our instructor was Ms. McChrystal. She was a very serious young woman with a full head of flaming red hair. Her mind was also full, it seemed, with the belief that her English course was the only one like it in the world. Unfortunately, she and I were not on the same page—literally. I proudly submitted my first assignment, and it was returned with more red ink than the original black ink. The red ink was as bright as her hair. Ms. McChrystal never smiled and was, frankly, not very gracious in providing directions or extra help. Her only feedback was the terse commentary she marked on the paper itself. I absolutely could not afford to flunk this course because it would impede my transfer goals. Sadly, I worked extremely hard to scratch out a D in her class.

I leaned on my Catholic faith and prayed, "Lord, if you'll just help me pass this course, I will do better next time. And I certainly won't take English II with Ms. McChrystal!" Well, my prayers were answered on both fronts. I finished the semester and then found an instructor who was far nicer and more understanding of my limitations. That was Mr. Summers. Through his teaching, I really discovered that there was something wrong in the way I processed information when I tried to write it down. This impeded my ability to learn. I could not exactly identify or label what I was experiencing, but I absolutely understood that I was still very skilled in speaking. So to improve my comprehension problem, I would say my thoughts into a tape recorder. Then I would write down whatever I had learned through the playback.

A Princess, Queen, and President

Really, this enjoyment of the spoken word stemmed from watching how active my parents were in the Latino community. My father was always invited to speak at social and community affairs. He easily demonstrated his bilingualism and melodic command of Spanish. Luckily, I was also bilingual, and Spanish had been my first language. So he strongly encouraged me to be comfortable with stepping in front of a microphone and speaking to crowds.

"*Mija*," he said, "don't be afraid. Embrace this opportunity. When you are in front of a crowd, you are in command. Know your subject, stand with confidence, and speak with conviction."

I didn't speak too often in Spanish, but because my parents were involved in the Latino social scene, I was always invited to participate too. If an organization had a queen-type competition, my parents had me run for it.

I ran for queen of several organizations, plus my parents asked me to be involved with the San Antonio Charro Association. With that group, I was named a princess. But as often as I ran for queen of this group or that group, I usually did not win. I had to appreciate what I was learning through the experience.

Then in 1967, I was invited to represent the San Antonio Charro Association at the Feria de las Flores (Fair of the Flowers) gala. My father had been selected as the Rey Feo—satirically, the Ugly King—of fiesta the previous year, and the year he was to give up his crown, I was to represent the San Antonio Charros.

For us ladies, on the night of the event, our escorts were young men from the Green Berets. I wore a shimmering *chapaneca* dress from Jalisco, Mexico, with embossed gold roses on a black background. There were fourteen nervous girls in this competition.

As the music began to play for my turn to enter the competition salon, I recognized that it was a very lively song called *La Negra*. Whereas the other girls strode elegantly and slowly into the room, I spontaneously switched up my entrance. I purposefully and joyously danced my way in.

The crowd stood, applauded, and cheered loudly, and I owned that atmosphere! That moment was sustained through the night, and at the conclusion, the judges named me queen. It was my first time ever being named queen.

That evening I wore a crown of flowers and greeted the nine hundred guests in attendance gratefully and happily. I was then asked to give an impromptu acceptance speech. Feeling too giddy to be nervous, Papa's words came to mind and I spoke with clarity and conviction. From that night on, because of that title, I had to frequently speak in public. That was when I realized that truly, my strength was in public speaking and most definitely not in writing.

This also made me hearken back to a few years earlier, when I was involved with an organization called the International Sorority. Our purpose was to raise money for research being conducted on muscular dystrophy. We were a group of high school and college young women who would put on a yearly fundraising event. These funds were sent to Jerry Lewis in New York in his quest to help those with muscular dystrophy.

Serving as president of the International Sorority on two separate occasions, I remained active with them as I entered San Antonio Junior College (and graduate school too). It was important to me to offer up my spare time in the name of muscular dystrophy research.

This also continued to strengthen my public speaking ability. In turn, I would utilize those skills in school to minimize my other academic weaknesses. Some have asked if I blame the nuns for not recognizing my limitations, but I do not. I believe they did everything they could to help me be successful. But I do wish those challenges would have been identified earlier because it would have been much less of a struggle in school.

Working tirelessly, I earned a certificate of completion two years later from San Antonio Junior College. As I had intended, I then applied to Our Lady of the Lake University. In selecting an intended major, I originally thought I wanted to be a speech teacher. But then I became intrigued by an advertisement for speech therapy. Although I did not have a speech impediment, I did have overall learning issues. So the study of speech pathology certainly piqued an interest. Plus, the university's program in speech pathology was nationally recognized. This convinced me to intently pursue this as a career.

I was admitted and began my studies in my junior year. It was 1966, skirts were getting shorter, Vietnam was more prominently in the news, and I was ready to work toward a Bachelor of Arts in the Science of Communication Disorders with a minor in psychology. As progressive as that era was becoming, it was still an all-girls school, and for the most part, the instructors were nuns. Depending on the major, there were a few laypeople too.

It was truly a busy time for me each and every day. In the mornings, as the air was still crisp, I faithfully attended classes. In the afternoons, when it would inevitably get a little warmer, and many of my classmates would head to diners and other fun places, I worked. I made a beeline to Franklin's Department Store because I was earning money to help my parents with my tuition and books. Education and supporting my parents in supporting me were my top priorities.

New Rules

I loved Our Lady of the Lake University. I was understanding my limitations with regard to reading comprehension and memorization a bit better. And this helped me enjoy my studies overall.

By December 1968, when San Antonio was glowing with Christmas lights and holiday songs filled the city's frosty air, I completed my studies. However, there was a problem: we were told by the university we could not receive our teaching certificate in speech therapy until we'd completed a master's degree. This was a new rule, apparently, and I was as surprised as I was mad.

Fortunately, my parents taught me to always be creative in seeking solutions. The university offered me a fellowship, primarily because they had extra funding. Instead of stewing over this surprise requirement, I accepted the fellowship. It allowed me to remain at the university and complete my master's degree in speech pathology within two years.

Upon graduation in 1970, I went to work for the Edgewood School District in San Antonio as a speech therapist. On my first day, I confidently strode into the personnel office.

"Good morning," I said, "I'm a new speech therapist." I reached into my file folder, expecting that they would want to see my transcript.

"Please follow me," I was told abruptly.

Without a further word, I was whisked upstairs to the office of Dr. Otillia Didaurri, who was in charge of special education. I was introduced to her and Mr.Carlos Contreras, the assistant superintendent for instruction. On the spot, I was offered a position with a grand sum of $396 per month.

When I got home and told my parents, they were proud that I was now gainfully employed but aghast at the tiny salary. My father was very direct: "The Edgewood School District now has an employee with a master's, who is in high demand—and that is *all* they will pay you?"

I saw that he was incredulous and placed a hand on his shoulder to calm him. Looking at him square in the eye, I said, "Daddy, these students in Edgewood *need* me.

Honestly, without my help, they will not get these services."

He looked over at my mom, who was also grimacing but had a slight trace of a smile on her face. Daddy took a deep breath, sighed, sat down in his recliner, and said, "OK. Let's see where it takes you."

CHAPTER 4

Don't Ever Tell Judy 'No!'

I Said Yes

My first few weeks in Edgewood felt abnormal. The assistant superintendent assigned me to go meet my first principal, Mr. Coronado. He was so glad to meet me because he saw I spoke English well and he needed someone to answer his telephone. That did not sit well with my boss, who proceeded to tell Mr. Coronado that I was not a secretary. He asserted that I was a speech pathologist that would be working with students who had speech problems on Mr. Coronado's campus.

Mr. Coronado then took me to a classroom that had chairs stacked up against a wall. This wall had a hole big enough that I could have fitted my entire body in it. Talk about natural air conditioning! I also discovered there were no supplies, so I brought materials from home. I set up my classroom and was officially ready for my new assignment. I returned to the district office one more time because I also had an office there. I also needed to meet the director of speech services. This was Ms. Lila Caldwell. She was a somewhat larger woman who was seated at her desk when I walked in. She was eating a snack.

We exchanged pleasantries, and then she pointed to a desk on the right side of the room. Apparently, this would be my desk. Ms. Caldwell simply said, "Good luck." Thus began my journey as a speech therapist in the Edgewood School District. It didn't last long.

Four months later, I was called into the superintendent's office. He wanted to ask me if I was interested in developing a program for preschool children with disabilities (back then, the societal term was *handicapped*), ages zero to eight. The district had received a grant from the Bureau for the Handicapped, and they needed a program developed. He felt that since I was a speech therapist, I would have the necessary skills to do this. I was not so sure. I had never been a school administrator, had never written a curriculum, and had certainly never developed a project. But I have a strong personality, and I really didn't have a fear that I *couldn't* do it. So I said yes.

Surprisingly, he offered a pay raise—from $396 per month to a grand total of $10,000 per year. I was ecstatic and could not wait to tell my folks.

I was assigned to a classroom at H. K. Williams Elementary School, where Ms. Pauline Key was the principal. Upon meeting me, she gave me a classroom out in the barracks. As very exciting as this was, something was missing.

"Ms. Key," I asked, "how come I haven't received any information on who I'll teach?"

"That's simple," she replied. "We don't know who needs these services. So right now, you don't have any students. You'll have to go out and find them."

I was stunned. And then, I collected my thoughts and turned them into a strategy.

And that's exactly what I did. I found eight students, up to age eight, who were in need of special services. Two of my most unique students were kids who had, respectively, autism and Down syndrome. Previously I had never worked with a child with autism, and I had limited experience in working with students with Down syndrome in language therapy.

I set up my newest classroom. But then I made another vital decision: I decided I could not do this alone. I began to require that parents come into the classroom one day per week for as much time as they had available. This helped me in working with the children. I named it the parent program.

We had funding for five years, which allowed me to oversee the development of a parent-involvement curriculum, a process for assessment and intake for students coming into the project, the curriculum of instruction, and training for teachers new to the project.

It was truly an amazing time. I taught, but because I really had no formal training in these areas I was developing, I learned so much too. We ended up with a project that included seven teachers, seven professionals, an evaluator, a secretary, and a parent liaison worker. The

Bureau for the Handicapped, a top federal agency, cited us as a model project. That opened the door to us consulting all across Texas, helping other districts develop their programs for preschool students with disabilities, ages zero to eight as well.

During this time, I began working with a former client of mine, Dr. Sylvia Little. We undertook the development of a manual to assist parents in working with their children as early as birth. We called it "Parents as a Child's First Teacher."

After we connected with the Independent School District of Brownsville, Texas, they ultimately contracted with us to write a curriculum for parents to use in helping their students develop language skills. Many weeks were spent in that school district researching and going to various places to identify things parents could do with their children that would be beneficial and not cost any money. Financial considerations were important. We got the manual written in both English and Spanish and proudly presented it to the district upon completion.

Educator or Thief?

After completing the development of the project at Edgewood Independent School District, I was offered the position of director of special education for the entire district. I confidently and gratefully said yes.

At the tender age of twenty-five, I was probably the youngest person in that type of position for a major school system in the entire United States. Naturally, I knew there were daunting challenges ahead in taking on such responsibility, especially at such a young age. But I also knew it would teach me well and provide crucial preparation for future administrative roles. I truly believed in enjoying the present while also planning for the future.

Though my time in Edgewood was certainly exciting, it was also a true learning experience. For example, we were temporarily housed in a new building named for a past superintendent of schools.

Dr. Jose Cardenas, the current superintendent, asked, "If we can repurpose this facility, would you be able to use it for providing services for special needs children?"

I said yes. What I didn't know was, at that time, the board of trustees were unhappy with Dr. Cardenas. And they already had plans on repurposing that building for other intentions.

That began a living nightmare for me. Demonstrations erupted, with angry protestors carrying signs in front of the district's central office. Some of those signs read JUDY LOREDO—EDUCATOR OR THIEF?

I was incensed, angered, and hurt. I was absolutely an educator. And most certainly not a thief. In fact, I was working extremely hard to ensure Edgewood was providing quality education for its students. Yet my life was threatened. I even had to have someone provide security to protect me from harm! They had to stay with me at all times.

Eventually, my parents hired an attorney to bring charges against a local woman who had led the picket lines. An injunction was awarded, preventing her from publicly calling me "Educator or Thief?" ever again.

I learned that you have to stand up for what you believe is right. But there is a price to pay. People will treat you wickedly and say vile things. I also learned that one should never slander individuals or cause others to believe that someone is unethical just because there is disagreement, be it educational, political, or otherwise.

Time for a Change

That was easily the most draining aspect of my two years on the job. Enduring that and looking at my long-term goals, I knew after two years that it was time for a change. It was time to go back to school and earn my Ph.D.

I was especially interested in the doctoral program at the University of Texas. In researching the program, I saw it would require me to commute from San Antonio to Austin for an evening class in the first semester. That was because the university had a special program to train individuals who wanted to be school superintendents. This Superintendent Training Program was run by Dr. L. D. Haskew and seemed like a golden fit for my goals. Unbeknownst to me, at the time, there were no female superintendents in the entire state of Texas. Between that fact and my young age of twenty-seven, when I met with the program's decision-makers, they were very visibly skeptical.

One even said, "Young lady, I admire your moxie but does a woman, especially a woman of your age, really expect to be accepted into this program? And then somehow get offered a job as superintendent? In my view, the answer is already a big fat no."

Well, don't ever tell Judy no!

I stood my ground and insisted I deserved to be considered. They allowed me to apply.

The application process went on for three grueling days in Austin, the state capital. We engaged in interviews and other activities with the statewide commissioner of public education, deputy commissioners of public education, independent school district superintendents from Dallas and Houston, and other school administrators.

The program was so new it had only accepted one other cohort, so twenty-five of us were applying for the second one. I was intimidated by the caliber of the other applicants, plus the fact that only ten would be accepted. But I didn't let that intimidation show, nor did I let it deter me. I charged ahead, believing I was just as good.

After the seventy-two hours of whirlwind interviews, a few weeks passed.

One afternoon I opened my mailbox. I was accepted into the University of Texas superintendent doctoral program. I did it!

Don't ever tell Judy no!

CHAPTER 5

Wake-up Calls

Pity Party of One

The late 1970s saw my life change pretty drastically. I was married. We had a daughter. And by the summer of 1977, I had a thirty-hour weekly internship at the State Department of Education and had been accepted into the doctoral program at the University of Texas. Changing my mind about commuting from San Antonio, I moved to Austin in August. I had never been away from home, and it was doubly hard leaving my husband and little girl. I was moving to a town where I knew not a soul. I had my studies and the internship in which I reported to Deputy Commissioner Dr. Jim Kidd.

The cohort into which I had been accepted consisted of ten graduate students, including me. Five of us were minorities, and five were Caucasian. It did not take long for the feeling that I was in over my head to envelop me like the Texas heat. But I refused to just turn around and leave as a failure. I did not want to quit on my parents, nor on so many others who had provided opportunities for me to advance in administration so quickly.

As I began my classes, I decided to circumvent this overload by taking a statistics course as a self-paced, study-at-home deal. It seemed like a wise move until I got back my first exam. It was a big, fat F. I sat in my apartment after receiving that grade and cried my eyes out. There *had* to be a way to pass this course. Failing was unacceptable. I knew two things for sure: I would have to work tremendously harder. And I absolutely felt like a lonely, overwhelmed failure. So I gave myself permission to spend some time wallowing in sadness. It was a pity party of one. As I began to feel sorry for myself, I poured myself a mixed drink. Up until that point, I did not drink much hard liquor, but my father had given me some in case I ever had company at the apartment. Then I turned on some slow, sad music. Sitting down with my drink and melancholy tunes, I sipped and sang and cried. The thought occurred that I had only eaten a bag of potato chips in the past two days. Waving that off as quickly as we waved off mosquitoes in the summer, I poured myself a second drink.

The next thing I saw…was my bedroom ceiling.

I woke up in bed in my pajamas. The phone receiver was lying on the floor. A muffled but desperate voice could be heard through the phone. It was one of my new girlfriends calling out, "Judy! Judy! Answer the phone, honey!"

Slowly I came to, but there were two poundings—my head and someone at the door. Trudging to answer it, I discovered it was another girlfriend, her sister actually, who came to check on me. She too had called, and apparently, all I did was mumble over the phone. Alexander Graham Bell would not have been proud! Neither was my friend's sister who looked aghast and asked, "What on God's green earth did you do to yourself, sugar?"

Quickly I replied, "Nothing that a little sleep can't cure." I say *quickly* because I then dashed to the bathroom. I vomited ferociously, a hard combination of alcohol and no food. Shaking as bad as a Texas tornado, I remained in this condition well into the next day. That led to the embarrassing act of calling in sick to school and work. I had never been that sick my entire life. Eventually, a good dose of rest, food, and self-reflection propped me back up. When I felt like myself again, I called my daddy and was honest with him about my pity party gone awry. He, too, was unimpressed, saying, "Well, I just hope you did not humiliate yourself in front of anyone."

"Oh, no, Papa," I earnestly replied, "I was by myself until a friend sent someone to rescue me. But I *assure* you I will never drink on an empty stomach again."

He muttered, "*Hmm.*"

Then I added, "And I certainly will never drink to the point where I do not know who or where I am."

My girlfriends' wake-up calls were a life lesson wake-up call. Never would I feel that sorry for myself or indulge in self-destructive behavior like that ever again.

Massive Undertaking

Score one for resilience. I worked harder in that statistics course than any other in my lifetime. And I passed it. The first semester ended well, and so did the following ones. Proudly I'll tell you that by the time I finished my coursework, I had earned all A's. This was with a thirty-hour-per-week job and a doctoral load of eighteen hours. I heard whispers, some internally and some by others who were doubtful: *No, Judy, this is just too much for you.*

But I renewed my focus. My goal of completing my Ph.D. was still in my crosshairs.

My first step was to get to work on my dissertation. That's when, one day, I was suddenly called into Dr. Kidd's office. He wanted me to meet with him and my doctoral chair, Dr. Ben Harris.

Dr. Kidd told me that he wanted me to evaluate the one thousand school plans that were being submitted, as they were yearly, showing the in-service education to be offered to teachers in the school system.

"Sure, I'd be happy to do that," I replied. "What evaluation tool will I be using?"

Dr. Kidd said flatly, "There is none."

Calmly and with a smile, I turned to Dr. Harris and said, "Well, sir, I guess that will be my doctoral dissertation. Since your expertise is in in-service education, I see this as an excellent opportunity to look at these plans and write up what I find."

He smiled too and simply said, "Judy, go for it."

Certainly, hindsight is 20/20, and I did not know then what I know. I was engaging in a massive undertaking! But I was genuinely excited.

In the end, my doctoral dissertation consisted of five chapters, over five hundred pages, and almost one thousand surveys and questionnaires sent to approximately 1,100 school systems across Texas. This was a mammoth project. But I learned the importance of having a strong tribe, especially my female support. To assist me in that project, I enlisted girlfriends I had met when I moved to Austin: Lilly Delgado, Elizabeth Gonzalez, and of course, Ginger (who had moved to Austin with me); my grandmother; and of course, my mother. They helped me prepare, stuff, and mail those one thousand envelopes. Yet I still needed to find someone at the state department who could help me with the tremendous task of analyzing and collating the data. I then needed to put that data into charts. I knew there was one way to accomplish this and get the help I needed.

A great challenge in all of this was writing the dissertation. Writing was one of my weakest skill levels because the nuns did not really help me improve on this. But hearkening back to when my parents encouraged me to engage in public speaking, I did feel quite comfortable with my presentation responsibilities.

So how did I handle the writing aspect? By enlisting Zively's typing service.

They typed and edited all my writings to help them appear more professional and reflective of a doctoral candidate. Again, it takes a village and a tribe, and even a good typing service.

Dr. Anderson Calling

My time at the State Department of Public Education was a true learning experience. Not only did I get to work with the assistant commissioner for professional development, I was also later assigned to Dr. Tom Anderson, one of the assistant deputy commissioners in the commissioner's office. I was granted that opportunity because I made quick gains in moving toward the completion of my dissertation in such a short time; they decided my second year should be spent with Dr. Anderson.

What an enlightening year! Seemingly every time I would go to class, I would get called out. The state department frequently wanted me to come back for a meeting or a task—all per the direction of Dr. Anderson. It really got to be a joke with my fellow doctoral students because whenever someone would enter the classroom with a message for our instructor, they would turn to me and say, "Dr. Anderson is calling."

My two assignments left me with no regrets because my experience with those two individuals blessed me so much intellectually and personally. The contacts they provided me were also tremendous, leaders like top state superintendents Billy Reagan in Houston and Linus Wright in Dallas. There was also Dr. Nolan Estes who was running the program at the University of Texas once Dr. Haskew retired.

During my doctoral studies, I was also able to meet and get to know the commissioners of education overseeing the state's education system. It was all such a monumentally draining but wonderful experience. In May of 1980, I received my doctoral degree. My parents, family, mentors, and friends were all so thrilled—and so was I. But I always kept one eye on the future. In this case, the future meant seeking out a full-time job. Immediately, I sought out leadership positions in public school systems. Quickly, the reality hit me. I was a thirty-one-year-old Latina with no experience in running a school system.

I was told no firmly and rapidly. The happiness of graduating from the University of Texas was soon clouded by the ending of my marriage. We both soon realized that our lives had taken different paths, him pursuing a medical school in Mexico and me a superintendent of schools position.

It was like hitting a brick wall.

CHAPTER 6

Making History

Not Going Backward

After earning my doctorate, I could not find work in the education field. It was beyond frustrating. So I accepted a part-time job in the Austin Law Offices of Jesse Carillo and Andy Forsythe. Although I was not using my doctoral degree right away, I was grateful to have it. It provided an assurance that I would not be doing secretarial work all my life because, believe me, I did not have the requisite secretarial skills to be successful at that job. That type of work provided short-term employment, but it was not something I was trained to do.

After working for them for a short time, I was offered a position as a consultant in compensatory education back at the state department. Although I was grateful, it still was not what I was trained to do. You must maintain your focus on what you are trying to accomplish and keep your standards high in life and never allow yourself to be sidetracked or shortchanged.

So I paid a visit to Mr. Tony Costanzo, the personnel director for the North East Independent School District in San Antonio. It was reputedly an excellent school system, and I wanted to be a part of it. He interviewed me, and I felt it went well. Then he told me he could not put me in a position of the administration. What could be done, Mr. Costanzo said, was that he could hire me as a teacher, start me in their training program, and then move me into an administrative position the following year.

Calmly, I explained that I had already proven my skills as an administrator. I had taught for three years, developed a full program, and I had served as a director of special education in a major school system. "Tony," I said, "with all due respect, I have no intention of going backward."

Now what Mr. Constanzo did not know was that evening, I was being interviewed by the Southside Independent School District (ISD) for the position of superintendent of schools. I thanked him politely for allowing me the interview and said I would consider his offer and get back in touch.

My life was also rather tumultuous at this point. Prior to my interview with the North East Independent School District, I had just returned from Houston, where my father had gone for a triple-bypass heart surgery. I stayed at the hospital with my mother until the surgery was complete and saw my father the next morning. Then I jumped on a plane to have an interview with Tony Costanzo at North East ISD. After all that, I returned home in the evening to prepare for my interview with Southside ISD.

The next day flew by, and quickly, the sun dipped into the cold San Antonio January night. I promptly went home and put on a beautiful new suit, custom-made by my *tia*,

Jean Raiford. Then I drove to Southside ISD for the interview.

When I arrived, I saw there were four other candidates. All of them were men. As the last scheduled interview, I patiently waited until finally being summoned into a conference room. I shook hands with the board of trustees. They totaled six men and one woman. Genuinely, they did everything they could to make me feel at ease. Dr. David Smith started off with the first question, and to this day, I have never forgotten the exact words he asked: "Can you please explain your philosophical and pedagogical views of bilingual education?" All I saw at that moment, in my mind, like a Texas saloon with flashing neon lights, were the words, *Judy, you are in way over your head*!

Taking a deep breath, I steadied myself. I gathered my thoughts—first, silencing the negative ones—and decided not to worry about uttering a perfect answer. I did not know what type of answer they were looking for, so all I could do was give an honest appraisal of my ideas on bilingual education: how it should be implemented and what the desired outcomes should be for the students involved.

The next thing I knew, two hours had flown by! I sat in that interview chair for two hours!

Figuring that to be a good sign, I had the gumption to ask, as we were winding down, "I'm just curious, y'all, did my answer about bilingual education align with your values and views?"

Dr. Smith cackled and replied, "Judy, we've kept you longer than we have any other candidate. I guess it's OK for me to reveal that we fired the previous superintendent because of his views on bilingual education."

Startled, I said, "Oh my. What were his views?"

Another board member quickly chimed in, "The exact opposite of yours!"

Whew! I internally thanked my Texas stars and mentally made the sign of the cross.

Another board member then noted that it was past midnight, and there was one final and remaining question: "If we select you as our superintendent of schools, how long would you remain?"

Taking time to, again, carefully reflect before I answered, I realized I had no set reply for that. After all, I was only thirty-one, so I could not promise that I would retire from Southside ISD.

After pausing, I said, "I will be here as long as I can be effective and as long as I, as superintendent hired by you, have a good working relationship with you. But I will most certainly *not* remain if my time is not being spent benefitting students and improving the system."

They seemed pleased, and we exchanged warm goodbyes. I did not analyze the interview on the car ride home, though. It was nearing 1:00 a.m., and I was just dog-tired.

Watch Me

After an abbreviated night of rest, I awoke with this thought: *Oh my word. What if I get the job?*

I dutifully got dressed and drove back to my job in Austin. No one knew that I had interviewed for the superintendent's position at Southside ISD. Interestingly, in previous conversations with professors and such, the consensus was that it would be a good ten years before the first female superintendent in the state would ever be appointed. My answer to *that*, mentally, was *Watch me.*

Just a short while after getting to work, at 8:30 a.m., I received a call from Clifford Shook, the Southside school board president. He gave me the news: it was a split vote.

Now although an offer can be made on a split vote, customarily, a superintendent would not accept it. If half the people are for you, that means that half are against you, and that makes life extremely difficult.

Mr. Shook went on to explain that the reason for the split vote was not because of a lack of confidence in my ability but because of the fact that I had never held the position of high school principal. I would be going directly from the position of director of special education in a school district to the titular head as superintendent.

In a happy tone, he then said, "Congratulations, young lady. We would be honored to have you as superintendent of Southside ISD." He added, "Judy, I assure you, although we were split on our vote, if you accept the position, you will have our *full* support."

"Mr. Shook," I calmly replied, "I am honored by your confidence and the commitment of your full cooperation. I gratefully accept."

Clifford Shook then advised me that the board would like to meet with me again to discuss my contract, which would include the salary and benefits. I agreed to come in, and we set the date and time. We then finished, with him, knowing it was Christmastime, saying, "We'll see you when the district returns from the Christmas holiday. Congratulations again, young lady."

As excited as I was, I was careful not to tell anyone the good news. But I did allow myself to call one of my mentors, Dr. Nolan Estes, who said, "I'm thrilled but not surprised. I knew you would achieve what you are setting out to do."

The secrecy lasted all of twenty-four hours. By the very next day, my telephone was ringing off the wall. Newspapers across the state, from Brownsville to Beaumont and San Antonio to Sugarland, wanted to interview Texas's first *appointed* woman superintendent of a major school system. It was front-page news.

By the way, I emphasize appointed because there had been a woman in the valley who assumed the superintendent position vacated by her deceased husband and also because Dr. Lane Murray was a superintendent of schools for the Wyndam Independent School District, which was in the prison system and not the traditional public school setting.

My new position, without question, was a thrill of a lifetime. The attention was great to be sure, and I felt like a movie star even though I never had to play a role. I was even prouder that in the ensuing three and a half years I was with the district, the board votes were 7–0. To be able to have achieved that took a great deal of listening, leadership, and cooperation from an entire faculty and staff and ensuring that we were all working toward the same goal.

Early Challenges

My challenges were great but even greater was my phenomenal staff. Even better, there were a number of individuals who had previously worked with me and now wanted to come to Southside to do so again. One of those people was Larry Rourke, who had worked closely with me in Edgewood and whom I absolutely trusted to have my back at all times. In addition, I asked Dr. David Herrera to come and join the team.

I also hired Mike Zolkoski as principal of the high school in Southside ISD. Frankly, Mike and I were not friends but professional colleagues when we were in Edgewood, which made it even more gratifying that he specifically came out to Southside to meet with me in my new role.

"Madame Superintendent," he said, "I want to help you succeed. Allow me to run the high school for you."

It took a little convincing, but I knew Mike was earnest because he paid multiple visits and came prepared to show me examples of the quality of his work and what he would do to put Southside High School on the map. So I hired him as principal and will happily say that not only was he superb in that role but he also went on to later become a superintendent in several school districts both in and out of the Lone Star State. Mr. Zolkoski stayed but a short time in Southside before moving on as assistant superintendent in Gregory-Portland ISD.

My second hire as principal was Joe Arriaga. Joe did tremendously amid severe obstacles. For example, the buildings were old and in need of renovation. Really, we needed to add a new high school too. In either case, there was no money in the system to allow us to borrow, secure a bond, or finance a total redesign. All I could do was patiently wait.

After much deliberation and research, I asked the board's permission to issue a request for proposals (RFP) from local architectural firms to study our district and come up with a plan to put the facilities in proper shape. Once we were able to float a bond and show that the district had achieved a satisfactory rating, the RFP produced an area firm whose plans we really liked. With the full vote of the board, the architectural firm was assured that as soon as we could achieve a bond rating, we would award the contract to their firm for the total redesign of the system.

We were happily amazed that they accepted the offer and would await a start date at a later time. But shortly after that decision, we discovered a budget shortfall in the system.

We again put out an RFP asking for accounting firms to submit a proposal to be considered as the firm that would do a lengthy audit of the system and then potentially be awarded the contract as the accounting firm for the school district.

I advised the board that we needed to contract with an accounting firm that had no connections to our district or to me personally in order to undergo a lengthy audit. The audit firm selected by the board on a unanimous vote began their study, and after approximately four months, they announced the audit was complete and that they were prepared to render their findings. They asked if they could meet with me, and I suggested that we wait until we could also include the president and vice president of the board of trustees. They agreed, and we scheduled the meeting for the following day. I did not sleep well that night because I was concerned that since I had assumed the role of superintendent of schools, it seemed that every month, we had to borrow from the bank in order to cover payroll.

The assistant superintendent at the time, Mr. Harvey Stein, assured me that it was not because of any difficulty with the bank balance but, rather, that we did not get our check from the state until a different date within the month, and we had to borrow the money to cover salaries until we received the state payment and then pay the money back. But it was after the third time we borrowed the money that I became concerned. So there is no doubt in my mind why I was losing sleep the night before I was to get the results of the audit. I knew we had been borrowing money on a monthly basis and paying it back when we received the check from the state department. That was not a good way to operate.

The morning came rather quickly. The meeting began when the audit firm arrived, and we patiently waited on their report. There was, indeed, a shortfall of one quarter million dollars in the district. Yet there were no signs of embezzlement. So how could this be? This was how: no delinquent taxes had been collected in quite some time, and the previous superintendent had based the district budget on a yearly 100 percent tax rate. It was flawed. We concluded the meeting with the auditing firm, and they provided some suggestions on how we could proceed. A proper formal announcement was made to call an emergency meeting of the board of trustees, and we met to discuss our plan of action.

I then visited a local bank to attempt to secure a loan so that the district would not show a deficit. Based on the meeting held with the board, I was instructed to visit the local bank to attempt to secure a loan so that the district would not show a deficit. They promptly told me, "No, ma'am. That's just not possible".

Refusing to give up, I sought out several prominent businesspeople because we had to do something.

Otherwise, the district was in danger of losing accreditation from the state because a system can never operate in the financial state we were in at the time. These leaders advised me to write a letter to the bank president requesting an audience with the board of directors to discuss my request to secure a loan on behalf of the Southside Independent School District. I did so, and further, I indicated in the letter how much I was requesting to borrow and also how I intended to repay the loan.

The morning after, the bank president had received the letter, and I received a very pleasant phone call. It was the president of Southside Bank who told me that my request for a meeting with the board of directors had been approved. I notified our board of trustees and asked that the president and vice chair of the board, along with my assistant superintendent, attend the meeting with me.

I prepared a detailed plan to aggressively secure a company to collect our district's delinquent taxes. These monies would be sent to the bank as security for the note.

When it came, the meeting was a marathon three hours. Finally, they agreed to consider this plan. But there was one important question. "Doctor," the president of the bank board asked, "how long will you remain at the district?"

I replied that, quite frankly, I did not feel the awarding of such funds to the district should be contingent upon if I was there or not. After all, it was the district's board of trustees who was ultimately the fiscal agent and who would be responsible for the repayment of the note, meeting the guidelines as stipulated by the bank.

That probably was not the safest answer, or what they had hoped to hear, but it was as forthright and honest as I could be. If they turned us down, I at least knew I gave a truthful explanation. Later that afternoon the president of the bank board gave me a call.

Yes, he said, they would lend the district the funding based on the secure payment of all delinquent taxes. They would offer us a five-year payout and would reassess the yearly interest so that if the interest rate went down, we would not have to remain at the rate with which we began.

Hallelujah! This was such a big win for our district and, most importantly, our kids and staff.

Heard It Through the Grapevine

I then continued my employment with Southside, thinking that I had uncovered the last stone that might have been a bombshell. Unfortunately, that was not the case. I soon found out that personnel files were not in order. You could not tell the difference between the bus driver, the cafeteria worker, or the teacher.

So one afternoon, I placed all personnel files in a box. After I had done a careful review and found the ones not meeting state requirements, I drove up to Austin to the Texas Education Agency to meet with Ms. Maggie McCullough, director of certification. She helped me get emergency permits for the teachers that were not meeting the requirements so that I could ensure that all my personnel files were in order.

I also assumed the task of writing curriculum guides with the teachers because, at that time, there was not a standardized curriculum as we have today. I spent time with teachers in training sessions, teaching them how to write behavioral objectives so that we could develop the objectives of the knowledge that would be taught per grade level. As the old saying goes, this ensured that "the left hand knew what the right hand was doing." Essentially at this time, our staff did not realize what a third-grade teacher was teaching and what a fourth-grade teacher was teaching. That meant that when students moved through the pipeline, you could not be assured they had the necessary skills to make the move to the next grade level.

We spent over one-year writing curriculum guides so we could meet state standards for accreditation. I implemented an evaluation system in order to be able to evaluate not only staff but also the teaching faculty.

Starting my tenure in Southside was also difficult because the community had a strong allegiance to the previous superintendent. So in order to gain community support, I began to establish committees that oversaw the cafeteria, facilities, and worked with principals to ensure we had the support for the programs and changes we wanted to implement within the system.

One of the major pieces of advice I had received from Dr. Billy Reagan, then superintendent of Houston ISD was that I should do a weekly newsletter for the board of trustees informing them of issues or occurrences that had taken place in the district that week. That way, they would always remain informed.

My weekly newsletter was called the *Southside Grapevine News*. It was probably the best thing I did because it stopped all gossip or miscommunication to board members since every week, I was filling them in on the happenings in the district and my responsive actions.

Burn, Baby, Burn

My time in the Southside Independent School District was one of the most rewarding experiences of my life. Being in a small rural system, even though it was part of a major city, you got to know everyone quite well. But I experienced personal adversity too. I went through the toughest loss any person can endure when my mother passed away suddenly on the operating table on October 5, 1981. I also spent an average of seventeen to eighteen hours per day in the district, and truthfully, it affected my personal life. My major support system, my mother, was gone, and I was running a school system and trying to fulfill my role as a single parent. But I knew that because of my deep faith and because of the support from family and friends, I would be OK. After taking time to grieve the loss of my mother and marriage, I met a wonderful man. We gradually began to get to know each other. Our friendship turned into dating, which I felt could potentially lead to a serious relationship.

I completed the duration of my term, and after three and a half years, I made the huge decision to leave my position as superintendent of Southside Independent School District. I was ready to move to Austin and get serious with that wonderful man. The board was not happy that I was leaving but, at the same time, showed tremendous gratitude and appreciation for what I had done for the district.

Upon completing my tenure, I was given a beautiful going-away dinner where I was presented with a picture of the building that would be constructed and named in my honor, the Dr. Judith Ann Lozano Vocational Building! In 2016 the building was repurposed, and it is now called the Judith A. Lozano Professional Development and Assessment Center.

Two years after leaving Southside, the loan I had helped secure was paid off, and I was invited back for the burning of the note.

To watch that note burn.

CHAPTER 7

Thank You, Mama

A Prestigious Honor

March 1980 is when I began my new role as superintendent of the Southside Independent School District. Let me share one more thing about then completing my doctoral program that year.

One day, my administrative assistant, Irene Martinez, told me I had a call. It was from Dean Kennemar of the College of Education at the University of Texas. After exchanging pleasantries, he said, "I'm calling to let you know that you have been selected to receive the annual award as the distinguished graduate of this college, given in the name of Dean Carl Brendt."

So stunned that I was, believe it or not, speechless, I had to catch my breath. Then I replied, "Uh, Dr. Kennemar, are you sure you didn't call the wrong person?"

Chuckling, he said, "No, ma'am, I did not call the wrong person. You are Dr. Lozano, correct?"

"Uh, well, yes," I stammered.

"Well then, I rootin' tootin' know I called the right person," he said while laughing. "Congratulations, Doctor."

I thanked him and gingerly hung up the phone. A million thoughts ran through my mind like Texas tumbleweeds. I was shocked. I was ecstatic. And I also immediately thought about the sister in high school who said that *if* I could ever make it through a college or university, since I was not very bright, I'd have to pay *them* for a degree.

Frankly, as tough as I know I am, those words pierced my heart like a silver bullet for many years. But now, I was receiving a doctoral degree *and* the Twentieth Distinguished Graduate Award at the premier tier 1 university in the state, knowing that there were only two tier 1 institutions—with A&M being the other—of all the universities in Texas. I just wish that teacher could have seen me then.

Graduation came on a gorgeous day, May 7, 1980. Each college at the university has a separate commencement ceremony, and that Saturday morning, I sat on the stage beaming in my doctoral gown. Prior to the presentation of the award, Dr. L. D. Haskew, who had been one of my major professors in the doctoral program, said a few words about me.

I will always remember the words he said, which hold true to how I have operated as an educator all my life: "Judy is the kind of person who, if she doesn't have the answer to a question, will go and seek the answer. And rest assured, when she comes back to give you the response, you will think she had written the book."

For Dr. Haskew to have spoken about me as he did that day brought tears to my eyes because of the stature of educator that he represented at that university. After Dr. Haskew's words, Dean Kennamer of the College of Education presented the award, and I summoned everything my parents had taught me about public speaking to confidently deliver an acceptance speech.

"Mom and Dad," I intoned into the microphone as I gazed at them in the audience, "you taught me to be strong, resilient, and never take no for an answer. You made me believe that I could make a difference. You taught me that no matter what I chose to do in life, in doing so, I needed to be the best at what I did.

"Dad, you gave me two pieces of advice when I assumed my superintendent position. First, 'Give a person power, watch how he uses it, and you will know the kind of person they are. Power can be dangerous in a person's hands. Use the power you have been given to make life better for someone else and to make a difference with your being there.' The second thing you said was, 'When you climb your ladder of success, be cautious. For those that you step on as you are on your way up, you will meet on your way down.'

"I have tried to live by those two statements so that no matter what I am doing, I always think of the other person and know that whatever my decisions are, they will have a positive impact on their lives. You have made me believe that I can make a difference, and even though it was hard work in getting to where I stand today, I know that it is because of your guidance, support, and love. This award is for you."

Afterward, they greeted me with flowers and hugs and large smiles. Papa dutifully took a zillion pictures on his Kodak camera. Then my mother embraced me. With tears in her eyes, she said, "Mija, as much as we believed in you, we didn't expect all this. We knew you could get a bachelor's degree. But never did we expect you would also get not one master's degree but two! And then a doctorate—along with this prestigious honor. You always exceeded expectations, and no matter if you had struggles, you still kept going. You never let anything beat you down, and that has made us so proud."

With tears in *my eyes*, I hugged her tightly. My father then said, "Dry your eyes, you two! Smile for the camera!"

Saying Goodbye

Then commenced a period when my work started to garner community recognition, and that was incredibly humbling. The *San Antonio Express* named me as one of their Distinguished Women in the San Antonio Community. I was also offered membership in Leadership San Antonio, a community-based organization that is part of the city's chamber of commerce. Receiving their training into all aspects of local leadership, I then gave back by serving on multiple community boards.

Countless memories were created in my tenure at Southside. I can honestly say we did a lot of good for students, families, and the entire community. It was marvelously gratifying. But every Southern spring kicks off with fierce thunderstorms. And as much as the sun kissed my face, rain also hit my head.

My mother passed away suddenly in 1981 when I was barely eighteen months into my job. It was a devastating blow I think about daily. As I have mentioned previously, the commitment of schooling and then running a school district slowly eroded my marriage into divorce. And there was that school bond issue for the dilapidated buildings. So much adversity came at once; all I could do was lean on two of Mama's favorite scriptural sayings: "And this, too, shall pass" and "For every dark cloud God sends you, he will send one with a silver lining." I could feel in my lowest of lows, my mom reminding me to just carry on. Don't give up and carry on. Things will get better.

Things did get better, and it coincided with the timing of my leaving Southside. I was thirty-five and had achieved great personal success but wanted to take a step back and smell the Texas roses. So I resigned from my position and decided to move back to Austin.

Why Austin? Well, when God closes doors in our lives, he opens others. I mourned my mom's passing but knew I had to honor her by pushing forward. After the period of lamenting my failed marriage, I dated a gentleman named Eleuterio "Sonny" Loredo, who brought joy back into my life. He was a confident businessman and most generous not only to his children, family, and friends but also to the community in which he lived. Another important quality that I noted in him was how he treated my daughter, Alysa Denise.

On May 7, 1983, as I was leaving Southside and exactly three years after the University of Texas graduation day, I enjoyed another formal ceremony. Sonny and I got married.

Now the Southside board had been reluctant to accept my resignation. But the one who officially accepted the resignation letter and told the rest of the board they had to accept it was Sammy Kirby. She was the board's lone woman at the time of my interview and had broken that tie during the selection vote.

"Judy," she told me and an assembled audience, "I am so sorry you are ready to leave. But I'm excited for your future too. And the board is excited as well. So we would like to bestow an honor that most people don't receive until they are long gone or even passed away."

I had no idea what that could be. Sammy saw the puzzlement on my face, smiled, and folded her hands together. Matter-of-factly she said, "We would like to name the new vocational building after you."

My word was I stunned again, to the point of speechlessness!

The audience stood and began to applaud, and the board president at the time, Mr. Fernandez, walked over to me and presented me with a picture with a rendering of the new building. I was stunned again, to the point of speechlessness, and tears welled in my eyes. I was thankful to God that my daughter, my aunt, and my father were present to witness this once-in-a-lifetime event.

I looked to the heavens and said, "I sure wish you were here to see this, Mama."

Sonny Days

After moving back to Austin, I prepared for a new life with Sonny and my daughter. He did not want me to work, so I stayed home and enrolled my daughter in the eighth grade at St. Austin Catholic School. Before long, I grew bored inside the house. So I began taking cake-decorating classes, eventually learning how to make gum-paste flowers and wedding and groom's cakes.

This was enjoyable but, unfortunately, not very profitable. I had thought of starting a side business by baking pastries and selling them, but I knew that was not my forte.

However, my hubby had other ideas for my talents. He had me manage his rental properties.

Intrigued by the challenge, I soon saw that this was not to my liking. Oftentimes, people were late with their rent or skipped out on it altogether. Sometimes they even left their place in shambles, which I just could not comprehend. And of course, we were stuck cleaning it up. Looking to the heavens again, I said, "Mama, I don't believe all your sacrifices were made with the intent of me ever being a landlord."

I looked up to the sky one day after leaving a duplex that had been left in shambles and said, "Lord, help me find the way because I know this is not my calling." With Sonny's encouragement, he said I needed to find things to do in the community because he did not want me to hold a stressful or restrictive full-time job.

One of my routes was to send a letter to the governor's office since Austin was the state capital. Informing them that I had moved to the area, I included a copy of my résumé. Was there, I inquired, anything I could positively contribute to in the community?

The response of governor's office was swift and affirmative. Yes, they said, there were several organizations that could use my assistance and expertise. The next thing I knew, I was serving on the board of directors of Brackenridge Hospital, Laguna Gloria (art museum), and Ronald McDonald House. All three kept me intensely busy.

However, when one serves on a board, it is not necessarily just for their wisdom or experience. It's for their ability to contribute financially to that organization. Repeatedly I found myself asking Sonny for donations. He was extremely generous but then made it clear he wasn't just a walking ATM. I completely understood, and I really did want to serve somewhere where my expertise *would* be utilized. So after further networking, I was appointed by the Austin City Council to serve on the Civil Service

Commission. We oversaw the police and fire departments. For a full circle, I enjoyed that assignment.

Another enlightening volunteer effort was serving on the Umlauf Garden board. And when the Opera Society began in Austin, I was invited to participate. Unfortunately, my health conditions did not allow me to continue with those endeavors.

Then life had further changes in store. I became pregnant with my second child.

After a lengthy bed confinement, my husband and I welcomed a bouncing baby boy, Lloyd Eleuterio, into the world in 1988.

Huston-Tillotson Family

Soon after Lloyd's birth, I went to work for Huston-Tillotson, an Austin-area private and historically black college. I was their chair of education, dean of academic affairs, and dean of academic support programs.

Like at Southside, I knew we were markedly improving the community. To see so many students cross the stage with beaming faces because their education dreams had come true was just priceless. I also became very involved with a statewide group of deans of colleges of education across the state known as TACTE

—Texas Association of Colleges for Teacher Education

—and ultimately served as their president. Two years later, I became president of the Consortium of State Organizations for Texas Teacher Education.

Huston-Tillotson University was like a family. I enjoyed every day that I went to work at that institution. It provided me the opportunity to help develop the lives of young men and women who wanted to become educators. It also afforded me the opportunity to meet people across the state who served in my same capacity. Too I learned how to redesign our program into one of the most respected teacher preparation programs in the state. None of this would have been possible without the phenomenal staff I had the pleasure of working with and leading throughout the implementation of our program.

When I look back at my experience at Huston-Tillotson, I never dreamed that I would do some of the things I did. I even told my daddy one time, "Maybe you and Mama could foresee this, but it has exceeded my wildest expectations."

CHAPTER 8

Challenges and Aspirations

My True Calling

My time at Huston-Tillotson contained great challenges and many rewards. Mama did often say the best things in life were usually the hardest. For example, I received a presidential award for academic teaching from President Dr. Joseph T. McMillon's administration. As if that wasn't thrilling enough, I also received the Sears & Roebuck Teaching Award for Excellence awarded by the Sears & Roebuck Corporation. And one of the greatest honors was receiving the Piper Professor Award, awarded annually to only ten individuals in higher education by the Texas-based Piper Foundation. Each college and university is given the opportunity yearly to nominate one individual from their campus to represent them as their nominee for the Piper Professor Award.

That year, I had the opportunity of being selected by our faculty at Huston-Tillotson University as the nominee. The Piper Foundation then has a committee review all applications and reduce them to ten finalists. The individuals selected represent institutions in a variety of disciplines across the Lone Star State.

Really, receiving that award made me feel like I had found my true calling. My other jobs were wonderful, but

I felt a special passion for preparing educators for a career in public schools helping youth achieve their goals, desires, and dreams.

Also, during my time at Huston-Tillotson, I was asked to apply for Leadership Austin, a community-based organization created by the Austin Chamber of Commerce. This program trained leaders for nine months on civic involvement, and then upon completion, those leaders are expected to serve on boards, committees, or other capacities benefitting the community. That led me to successfully apply for Leadership Texas. It was similar but was a yearlong program teaching us about our great state's history, programs, and services—again, in service of others.

Adding to these honors was receiving the Academic Excellence Award from the Hispanic Chamber of Commerce, specifically for my contributions to Latino education in Texas. It was really quite prestigious because in this state, the local and statewide Hispanic chambers of commerce have just as much, if not more, influence than even the general community chambers. That's not the case in most of America.

Truly, I never expected these honors, awards, or commendations. And I didn't work specifically to receive these honors. But I firmly believe when you work hard, people will recognize your passion, skills, and results. Doors will open and awards may follow. Each time, I felt as thrilled as I did humbled.

Great Challenges

As fantastic as the recognition was, our challenges at Huston-Tillotson were also strong. The teacher education program was struggling. The accreditation process had changed, which we discovered we were not in compliance with, and we were facing the potential of losing that validation.

Two strengths I knew we had were an outstanding faculty and good relationships in the community with other teachers in the Austin public school system. So we teamed up the faculty with local teacher educators and redesigned our entire teacher preparation program. Not only that, we also revamped our criteria for admission *and* completion. This led to our program being reaccredited with no violations.

As chair of education, I also discerned that we needed to add a program to prepare individuals who already had degrees to receive something called an alternative teacher certification (ATC). With tremendous assistance, Dr. Alicia Moore—who was a graduate of our college in our department—designed, developed, and implemented the ATC program. Dr. Moore remained with the program for one year. Following her was Marguerite North.

Ms. North did a phenomenal job in launching the program and moving it forward. With both the traditional and alternative programs, deans considered these to be programs of high quality and productive too. We were producing educators who were successful and staying on the job.

After having served in that role as chair of the education department, a golden opportunity arose when the new president of the university, Dr. Larry Irvin, added the position of dean of academic affairs. There was also a new provost, Dr. Sandra Vaughn, who assumed her role under Dr. Irvin's leadership.

So I decided to apply for the new position of dean of academic affairs. After being interviewed by a committee, I was successful in that endeavor and worked alongside Dr. Vaughn, which truly was an honor and privilege. It was decided after I assumed my new role that I would also *continue* to oversee the department of education. Essentially I had a dual appointment.

That made it a difficult first year in that role. Also, unfortunately, Huston-Tillotson had been placed on probation by the Southern Association of Colleges and Schools, just as we were facing our ten-year study. There was so much work to accomplish because losing accreditation would have been devastating to the institution and to students currently enrolled or future-enrolled.

As I settled into the new position, I was responsible for overseeing the academic program and to ensure it would be reaccredited. So I incorporated appraisal systems, surveys (remember all those surveys from my doctoral dissertation), and accountability measures. We had to make certain we were successfully reaccredited.

Determined but also scared we would not be reaccredited, we engaged in five months of grueling work.

Finally, it was time for President Irvin and myself, along with key staff he invited, to journey to San Antonio—a city that already held so many emotional memories for me—to learn our fate. I prayed and hoped and just had faith we did all the necessary things. Adding to my anxiety was that this was the first time I had served in a collegiate higher administrative capacity. So this rectifying of our school's previous mistakes was squarely on my shoulders. Plus I knew that if we were *not* reaccredited, we would lose the right to award financial aid and continue to enroll students. This could lead to us shutting our doors.

Huston-Tillotson College was the oldest institution in Austin, even older than the University of Texas at Austin! For our doors to close would be a devastating blow to the community, especially African American families. Many individuals walked its halls, completing their education and then heading out into the world to make lasting impacts.

Dr. Irvin met with the accreditation board from the Southern Association of Colleges and Schools on that fateful afternoon at the J. W. Marriott on the historic River Walk in San Antonio, and ... goodness gracious— we were reaccredited with all violations removed!

Becoming a University

After the euphoria of cleaning things up and getting reaccredited, there was more work to be done. Major changes were on the horizon like clouds peering over a

Dallas or Houston skyline. Dr. Irvin and the board of trustees wanted Huston-Tillotson to become a university. This led to a whole new series of processes and preparations.

It really was difficult because Dr. Vaughn, whom I adored, had left, and Dr. Nadine Jenkins replaced her as provost and vice president for student affairs. Amid a very taxing year, we navigated all the changes. Then I was asked to be dean of academic support programs, as the dean of academic affairs position was dissolved.

Within my administrative roles, I was overseeing the development of the university bulletin, all faculty meetings, implementation of all registration processes, and development of degree plans that students were following through their advising process. My position was also responsible for the intake and implementation of orientation for all freshmen students. As an advisor, I counseled every incoming student in the teacher education program and assisted with budget development.

Those roles were tough, but the greatest challenge was when I was asked to develop the degree plan for criminal justice. I oversaw and developed the actual course descriptions and titles ultimately approved by the *Southern Association of Colleges and Schools.*

I really began to look at things with a long-range view in mind. We had aspirations to become a university, and I had worked there for two challenging but fulfilling decades. When would be a prudent time to perhaps do something else?

As those thoughts marinated, I developed a revised course numbering system for all courses listed in the college bulletin. I also continued serving on many committees on our campus and at the State Department of Education on behalf of our school. One day I was sent by our president to a meeting convened by the Texas Commissioner of Higher Education, Dr. Kenneth Ashworth.

At that meeting, I was thanked for my willingness to serve as one of the co-chairs for that year's commissioners' conference. This was an annual gathering where the commissioners of higher education and public education, respectively, came together.

That task was assigned to myself, Texas Higher Education Coordinating Board (THECB) assistant commissioner Dr. Glenda Barron, and State Department of Public Education director Dr. Delia Quintanilla. It was as challenging as I anticipated but also very rewarding, and I'm grateful to have had that opportunity.

Subsequently, I was asked to serve on a committee at the THECB, the agency that approved programs submitted by colleges and universities, to be forwarded to the higher education commissioner and board for their final approval. Eventually, I went from sitting on the committee to chairing it. This allowed me to meet so many university presidents and vice presidents of academic affairs from across the state.

Well, two great things then happened, one which we had been working toward, and the other was a complete surprise. We succeeded in turning Huston-Tillotson from a college to a full-fledged university. Everyone felt exceedingly proud. The other thing occurred as I was sitting one afternoon in my office. It is interesting and perhaps divine how certain surprises come your way. A phone call came in from a former Huston-Tillotson colleague who was working at the THECB. He wanted to let me know that a position had become available at the agency that seemed to have my name on it. The requisite credentials and experience matched all those that I had held. Initially, I was surprised to receive the call but then realized the opening fit everything I had accomplished or had experienced thus far.

Thinking more about it after the call concluded, I thought about how I felt ready for a change. I also still needed to accrue three more years of what was considered "best years of service" in public education in order to have an acceptable retirement base. But when would retirement be?

Was that a selfish motive? I gazed once more to the heavens, whispering, "Mama, should I apply?"

CHAPTER 9

We Have Liftoff

The Next Step

After much deliberation and prayer, I decided to apply for the position. Submitting my résumé and cover letter, I did so confidently. But then I did not hear back for quite some time. Then on a frosty December evening in 2007, I received a call from one of the executive officers at the Texas Higher Education Coordinating Board (THECB), Mrs. Linda Battles. She requested that I come in the following Monday to be interviewed by the commissioner of higher education, Dr. Raymond Paredes, for the opening.

It turned out I was able to do the following Tuesday afternoon. It was Dr. Paredes and four deputy commissioners who conducted the interview. Now I was used to long, marathon-session interviews since, if you recall, for my interview for superintendent at Southside Independent School District (Southside ISD), we began in the late evening and ran past midnight. But in this interview, they primarily asked only one question. It related to my view of the current state of higher education. Taking a moment to collect my thoughts, I then began to speak and did not stop. Really, I just ran with it, spoke from my heart, and said everything that I felt best supported my answer. I have always prided myself on being direct and speaking the truth. I will admit that the training my dad gave me in my early years regarding public speaking included always being able to speak and sound intelligent. That training served me well during this interview.

Commissioner Paredes heard me out, leaned back in his chair, and with a very serious look on his face, said, "Dr. Loredo, you paint a pretty grim picture of education."

Smiling, I countered, "Oh no, Commissioner, au contraire, if you look back at when I began my career in 1970, public education had no accreditation system that contained accountability, assessment, or even the basis for curriculum guides. Today we have all of these things in place."

I continued, "So every challenge we now face in higher education around developmental education and the preparedness of students to go to college will be a blip on the radar screen. There will be other challenges down the road."

They did not indicate if they liked that answer or not, but frankly, that did not matter to me. I knew I had answered honestly, forthrightly, and with examples to support my conclusion. My hope was simply that my values matched theirs overall.

The holiday season then floated by, with the traditional Texas samplings of bright lights, festive music, and tons of tamales. I adore Christmas, so I really paid it no mind in the passing weeks that I had not heard back about the job. Besides, I was very happy at Huston-

Tillotson; and if this position was not meant for me, so be it.

Then on New Year's Eve, I was lunching with friends. A call came in on my cell phone from Dr. David Gardner, the deputy commissioner of academic programs at the coordinating board.

I was afraid the call was to offer me the job. It was my first true realization that, if that were the case, after twenty-two challenging but ultra-rewarding years, my time at Huston-Tillotson really was coming to an end. Truly, I was not prepared for those types of emotions yet, so I left the call unanswered.

A week later, on January 7, 2008, as a bitter cold descended upon winter in Texas, Dr. Gardner called me at home. It was to offer me the position as assistant commissioner of P-16 Initiatives, which was one of the three divisions at the THECB. My initial reaction upon being offered the job: I broke into tears. Weeping over the phone, I thanked Dr. Gardner, who was very confused.

"Dr. Loredo, oh dear," he said, "I didn't mean to make you cry!"

Momentarily stopping my sobbing, I replied, "Oh no, Dr. Gardner! You just don't understand. You see, I haven't been offered a position by an outside agency in twenty-two years. I guess I'm just emotional, shocked, and very happy!"

We both laughed, and he wished me a Happy New Year. Then I accepted the position.

GenTex

The following day, I returned to Huston-Tillotson University and informed Dr. Earvin that I would be leaving. However, I committed to teach my classes until the university found my replacement. Both the university and coordinating board were gracious about that arrangement. Dr. Earvin was kind throughout the whole process.

He said, "Dr. Loredo, there was never a doubt in my mind you would be offered that position. You may not realize this, but over the years, you have developed many, many skills. Perhaps you don't recognize them, but I assure you, others do."

In the middle of January, I began at my new place of employment. One of the first things I learned was that several others had also held this position, none of them lasting more than a year. Daunted but not deterred, I was determined to find out why.

The prior assistant commissioner was Dr. Glenda Barron, whom I knew personally and who was now the president of Temple Community College in Central Texas. So I began by calling her, but she never returned my messages.

Suddenly, one day I saw her in Austin at a legislative session at the capitol. Politely but directly, I asked why she had never returned my calls.

"I do apologize, Dr. Loredo," she said, "but I simply did not want to taint you."

The following six months continued to be very hard, but I was blessed with an incredible staff, including a phenomenal administrative assistant, Mary Comerford. Seemingly there was just one landmine after another. But I got through them, thanks to my directors, Dr. Susan Barnes, Lynette Heckmann, Evie Hiatt (who ultimately became my assistant deputy commissioner), and many other incredible staff members.

So much was accomplished, including moving programs in developmental education forward, implementing a statewide campaign called GenTex for creating a college-going culture, and continuing the work involved in overseeing programs funded by the state and housed in the Division of P-16 Initatives.

The GenTex campaign, for example, faced many obstacles. But once we launched it, a good number of people embraced it. One of them was University of Texas quarterback Vince Young, who piloted the Longhorns to a stirring national championship in 2006. He invited me onto the television show he had in Austin and later asked me to speak at the annual gala for his charitable foundation. He loved that I specifically addressed the students who were in attendance that night and returned the favor by signing keepsake pictures for my grandsons and family. Vince was a remarkable athlete and an even better person who truly believed in the power of education.

Every time a hurdle frustrated me, I thought back to what Commissioner Paredes told me soon after I was appointed: "Dr. Loredo, we have no one in this agency that has the experience or credentials you have." This surprised me because I never considered myself to be much different than anyone else. But a compliment like that from a man of his stature made me realize I had a considerable amount to offer.

So I continued to dig deep and did achieve many things, thanks to Dr. Gardner who hired me and served as my immediate supervisor at the coordinating board for six years; Linda Battles and the agency's legal teams; two other wonderful assistant commissioners, Dr.

McGregor Stephenson in academic affairs and Susan Brown in planning and accountability; Dr. Gary Tomerlin; Dr. Stacey Silverman; Dr. Kristen Kramer; and Dr. Julie Eklund.

What a team!

Leaving a Legacy

All good things must come to an end, which is how I began to feel about this job and my overall career. We accomplished a tremendous amount. But I was already sixty-eight years old now. Retirement and family time beckoned.

Eventually I resigned my position and looked to transition into retirement, which was to be short-lived. I began a brief tenure at storied Texas State University, the state's oldest institution, which had existed in San Marcos since 1899 and was known for its preparation of educators.

I worked under the direction of Dr. Araceli Ortiz, who had been awarded a grant from NASA to look at curriculum in teacher education. The goal was to revise the curriculum used by teachers in public education so that it was more culturally relevant.

Knowing that I did not have a background in science, Dr. Ortiz still had faith in my ability to communicate with deans and work with universities across the state who would be invited to work on this project. Her confidence in me stemmed from when she and I worked together at the THECB when she created the model for faculty members in the field to begin to implement the college-going curriculum in the areas of science, math, English, and social studies.

The project funded by NASA at Texas State was the only one of its kind. My assignment was to work with faculty in high minority-serving institutions across the country and to coordinate the work they would be addressing in the project.

It was highly rewarding and just short enough to not swallow up my last bit of remaining energy. My work with the project was completed in August 2018, and I knew I was ready. I was ready to truly retire and enjoy my family and do the things I never had time to do. Of course, retirement for me is different from the definition probably held by many others. In many ways, I became busier than ever. Sonny and I began traveling and seeing the world.

Hearkening back to everything my parents did to improve their communities, I plunged into doing more community service in San Antonio. Along with my husband, I served as president of an organization called the Sembradores de Amistad—which translates to Sowers of Friendship.

This organization was originally founded by our neighbors to the south, Mexico, to be sowers of friendship between our two countries.

They included a community project, and ours was to raise scholarship money for first-generation students. Sonny and I began working with Sembradores way back in 1987 in San Antonio when we both served as presidents of that chapter. On November 25, 1994, we created a chapter in Austin with eight couples as the founding members.

After our tenure as leaders, my husband was designated president emeritus. We had begun our work to establish endowed scholarships at the four colleges and universities in Austin. Today those endowments, available to first-generation students, exceed over $150,000 each, and students may apply for them annually.

Adding to my busy retirement is currently serving on the Hispanic Chamber of Commerce Foundation Board of Directors. I was vice chair and am now the chairwoman. In line with the foundation's mission, I helped the organization implement events to raise money for scholarships, leadership training, and health and wellness for first-generation students.

For the last four years, I have cochaired the annual "Let's Win the Future" scholarship fundraising gala. All gala proceeds have been used for endowments implemented at local colleges and universities. I'm proud and humbled to say that in the past three years, we have established a $100,000 endowment in the College of Business at Texas State University and an $80,000 endowment at Austin Community College. This year we have begun to implement an endowment at St. Edward's University, with an initial check of $25,000.

Now prior to my assuming the position of chair, there was already an endowment at the College of Education at the University of Texas. My goal is to add another one that is university-wide there in Austin.

I have also served as a member of Wonders and Worries, an organization that raises funds to provide free counseling services, regardless of income, for children whose parents are suffering from a catastrophic illness. I served on their board for over three years and chaired their annual fundraising gala.

I was also asked to join the founding board of Con mi MADRE, an organization that assists middle and high school female juniors develop a relationship with their mothers. Along with those mothers, they also learn to develop the necessary skills to advance to college—and be successful there. Serving on that board for five years, I was incredibly honored to be given a Distinguished Award for Service in 2017.

In 2017 I also had the honor of serving as President-Elect (and eventually parliamentarian) of the Ladies Auxiliary at Barton Creek Country Club in Austin, Texas. Today I serve as chair of the Hospitality committee and Co-Chair of Discover Austin.

Yes, Sonny laughs at my idea of retirement. But I do also enjoy golfing, baking, and entertaining friends, and he and I have traveled to China, Africa, and most places in between. We have a very large family, keeping in mind I was an only child, and they provide the greatest joy. What truly gratifies me, though, is thinking back to the struggle of my parents as immigrants and as a young couple who were caretakers of my grandparents and aunt.

I think back to the nun who said I did not have the capacity to succeed. And I think about not only my successes and failures but about the way I have worked to ensure the success of many others. All of it just proves that with education and determination, you can mount any challenge. With education, you must be willing to serve and use your talents. And no matter what our limitations may be, we can and should make this world a better place. Anything is possible to those who believe.

I have lived by this saying, and I hope that in the end, I will have fulfilled every word: "You shall walk this way but once, and you shall make a difference, or your passing will have been in vain!"

CHAPTER 10

The Road Map to College Success

No one is born perfect, and all of us have our own qualities and faults. But remember, we are not defined by the faults; we are defined by what we do with the qualities that God has given us.

—Dr. Judith Ann Gutierrez Loredo

The Six Bs

What qualities are needed to be a prepared student who can be successful into post-secondary education?

Often I sit back and utilize my experience as a teacher especially, I think of what I should have done when I was beginning my middle school years leading to high school and then college. I might not have had as much difficulty as I did if I had realized the six B's, which are as follows:

1. *Be on time.* It is important that you learn at a very young age to be on time for class. It is just the same as having a job. Future employer will not want you to be late (or to leave, and it is no different for your teachers in your primary years through college. Teachers want you to be on time, whether you are staying in one classroom or between classrooms. When class begins, you need to be there.

2. *Be prepared.* Nothing is more annoying to teachers than begin the class and find out students have not done their assignment, whether it was reading or preparing a project. When you are not prepared, the teacher has to go back and spend class either re-explaining the material or modifying the lesson last minute so he or she can move forward with the day. This is the material that you should have brought to be able to discuss or show to the class.

When you are not prepared, it means it will be one day longer in going on to the next assignment or moving on to the next lesson. You have no time to waste because—guess what?—in your college years, your professors will not wait on you!

3. *Be attentive.* It is absolutely exasperating to the teacher and other students when someone is not paying attention. Today, some of the biggest distractions are students texting, mailing, or looking at their social media on their cell phones when the teacher is trying to teach.

I do not know any student who can engage and multitask while trying to learn new material. You must be attentive to the discussion and to what other students are asking or what is being explained because for every moment you become distracted, you are missing a piece of the puzzle of the material you are trying to learn.

When you go home, it should then come as no surprise when you do not know how to complete the assignment or even how to begin the assignment because you were not fully attentive during class.

4. *Be a notetaker.* If you do not know how to take good no class, I suggest you go online and look at the many examples of how to take notes. It does not matter what you are in. You should have notes for every class to summarize or refresh your memory about what the teacher in class or what you may have read in the book. Your notes will help you prepare not only for class the next day also for exams in the future. They will also enable you to be on time, prepared, and attentive.

5. *Be a participant.* The teacher in your classroom has been to school, and his or her role today is to teach you material of the course you are taking. If you are in school, you may stay in the same room or have different classrooms throughout the day. Whatever circumstance, be a participant in the class you are in. Show that you have read the material being discussed. That you understand the material, and do not wait for a teacher to call on you simply because you do not want to answer questions or provide information.

Do not be ashamed if you cannot answer a question or do not understand what the instructor is teaching. It is to your advantage to be truthful! Get your questions answered! That is infinitely better than to just sit there and appear as though you do not care.

6. *Be an initiator.* Teachers respect students who serve as leader or who step forward to answer a question. They respect who comes to the blackboard at the front of the class to present. Does that intimidate you? Well, the only way to overcome your fears is to step up to the plate, swing fences, and show what you know!

As I think back about myself as a student, I know I did not follow all the B's shared here.

I was on time, and I always did my homework, but I know that I was not the best notetaker. That was because I did not understand what was important to put down or what was needed to do well in the class. I always wanted to participate, but unfortunately, many times, I was not called upon. I always felt that it was only the bright students the teachers wanted to hear from and maybe not from me because I wasn't considered bright. I even felt like some teachers had their "pets," and I was not one of them. So, therefore, I just sat in class and was quiet so that I would not be called upon.

If I could do it again, I would do what I have just recommended to you because, as a teacher and college professor, I understand now that those are the actions that will enable you to be a successful student in whatever grade you are in or course you are taking. I also realize now that if I call upon the same students, I am making others feel less valued. A good teacher will always take whatever answer a student gives and try to find something in the answer that responds to the question. I always felt dumber when a teacher would haltingly say, "No that is not correct!"

Foundation of Strength and Passion

Build a strong academic foundation. Your academic foundation consists of the courses contained in the academic track you have selected, whether you are in middle school, high school, or college.

In high school, you will be given options of the track you want to follow. Please learn early on that you must continue some type of schooling beyond high school. High school is not the end of your formal learning.

Research shows that to have gainful employment, you must have skill training beyond high school, whether it be technical training or a college degree. Whatever it is that you choose, you must strive to be the best. You must know who you are as a student, and most importantly, you must know your passion. It is very difficult to learn any material when you do not know your passion, interests, or even learning style.

As far as learning styles go, not everyone can learn by listening and absorbing information. Not everyone can learn by just reading the material either. In fact, many students of color are multisensory learners, which means they must hear it, see it, read it, write it, and discuss it in order to absorb the material completely.

Sit back and think about yourself as a student and ask, "How do I best remember the information I have learned?" That is then connected to understanding your passion. Many times, you will hear students say things like, "Math is hard ... Science is boring ... I don't like anything I do in school." Au contraire! There is something that you enjoy, but you just do not realize it.

In the adult world, everything is not divided, so you don't do mathematics first and then science and then reading. All of it is part of a daily routine. So what is it that you really enjoy? Because understanding that is what will help you the most in making the decision about which track you should consider pursuing in high school.

Grades Matter

We sometimes don't realize how important grades are until it's too late. I did not understand when I was younger that grades from middle school and high school would be carried with me and that the college I applied to would look carefully at the grades I made in my high school subjects.

My advice to you is to realize very early on that grades do matter. You do not have to be a straight A student to be successful in life. In fact, those are the students who many times find it difficult to be successful once they enter higher education or the workforce. But the student with decent grades, a variety of extracurricular activities in their academic and personal lives, and who is involved in school activities is a more rounded student. He or she will find greater success as they move through their college years.

Good grades aren't the only thing, but they are a very important thing.

Qualities Needed to Be a Successful Student

As I think about the students I have taught, as well as myself as a student, I can see that there are certain behavioral descriptors that every successful student demonstrates. They are the following:

1. Drive
2. Initiative
3. Conscientiousness
4. Applied
5. Studious
6. Leadership

These qualities are numbered here, but they are not intended to be listed in any order of importance because each can stand alone. Grouped together, these are behaviors successful students demonstrate.

Drive

Every successful student is driven to be better at who they are and what they do. They think about themselves as a student, they consider their future, and they move forward in an organized fashion in order to ensure their success.

Initiative

Successful students do not wait to be told what to do next. They are always prepared to move forward without, in many cases, much guidance. They are also not afraid to make a mistake and to ask for help along the way.

Conscientiousness

A conscientious student is one who follows the six Bs leading to success. They are also the students who have learned how to manage their time and complete tasks they have been asked to do or activities they are involved in. They have a sense of responsibility for their actions and understand how their actions affect others.

Applied

Apply yourself! To be an applied student is to face the challenges, do the work, and be willing to accept constructive criticism and failure as you move through the academic years.

Studious

You have to be studious and not lackadaisical. No matter the grade level, a student who studies is a successful student. You cannot expect to attend class, listen to the teacher, participate just a little, and then go home and not reopen a book to review what you learned in class—or to complete assignments.

Good students can separate having fun from studying and understand that they study in order to be able to play.

If you do not study and make the grades, as the interscholastic sports saying goes, "no pass, no play." The most important tasks you must complete while in school are to attend class regularly, do your work, do your best, and be proud of what you have accomplished. At the end of the year, this should lead you right into college.

Leadership

This is defined as being the student who is respected and who other students want to emulate or be like. People who have leadership qualities are followed by other individuals, although that may not always lead to a positive outcome in every situation. But when we talk about your preparation as a student, leadership in this sense shows that not only can you handle the work assigned but that you can take on other tasks and be successful in every endeavor you undertake.

Get Involved

Look, it would be a very boring life if all we did was go to school, study, do our work, and return the next day to begin the same routine. Students who seek involvement in activities outside the classroom tend to be more successful and well-rounded individuals.

When you have completed your formal education, not only will a college look for extracurricular involvement, employers will do the same. The message it sends is you have interests beyond the classroom. Get involved socially or civically in your community. This is what it means to be a well-rounded and balanced individual.

There are other things to consider if you are to be a successful student. Be prepared for class with a pen or pencil, paper, and most importantly, your textbook and any other required material. Ask and answer questions. To sit and not be involved is not a sign of a successful student. Have a notebook to keep track of assignments for each day and to remain organized, and keep track of what and when is due in each class. Most importantly, keep careful track of when exams are scheduled.

Now one of the first things a teacher gives you—even in middle and high school—is an outline of the course. That outline should be read carefully and followed because it is like a contract between you and your teacher for the course. It will usually contain information about the class, including goals and objectives, and what the teacher is hoping you will learn. It may also explain the class rules and how to reach your instructor. That document should be kept somewhere so you can refer to it as needed and should never be lost.

Make Those Connections

School is a place where you form new relationships. Many people forge lifelong relationships with those they attend school with. Making friends also helps build connections with potential study or learning groups, which can help you to be successful. You will benefit in classes by bouncing course information off each other or discussing material and asking questions. Utilizing a group environment helps to strengthen your understanding of the material you are learning because you can get perspectives from different types of learners.

Advanced Placement

Let's discuss Advanced Placement and Pre-Advanced Placement (AP and Pre-AP) courses. It is important in your primary years leading to your collegiate years that you do not shy away from taking difficult courses. Be sure to challenge yourself because it is not going to get any easier as you move through your formal education. In fact, it will only become more challenging, especially when you get to college. This is because you are being prepared for your career and future work in life. To only take the easy way out and not take advanced classes may also send a negative message to college admission directors. Students with AP credits on their transcripts and who have taken collegiate-level high school courses for dual credit send a positive message to any college admissions office.

Technologically Speaking

Another important area today is the world of technology. From early on, you were introduced to computers, iPads, cell phones, and more. Each can be invaluable tool to help you learn the material and even study. Also, do not shy away from taking a typing course because it is much easier to use a computer if you have mastered using a keyboard without having to search for letters. Use just one or two fingers to type. The more technologically savvy you are, the better student you will be in your collegiate or graduate school education. You need to learn word processing, spreadsheets, presentation programs, and others because you will have to utilize them throughout your education. Students in elementary schools are already using presentation software, and much of the information they use in class is accessed via the internet.

Final Thoughts

At times you must pass through difficult roads in order to get to a wonderful destination. But everything you do along the way helps you to be a better traveler and student. As you awaken in the morning and go to school, whether it's high school or college, every day should be seen as an opportunity for you to be better. Consider each day as one of the best days of your life. Every day is important. Every day matters. Every minute matters.

There will be times when you may feel that you can't go on, but keep the faith! Know that the next door will open for you to walk through. Sometimes we must experience failure or adversity in order to get to success. Always remember that success is failure turned inside out. I failed many times along my road of life. I was disappointed many times. I found it hard sometimes to pick myself up to keep going on, but I never lost sight of what it was I was trying to accomplish.

Everything will not go your way all the time, and in fact, more often than not, things do not go as smoothly as you would like. But keep in mind that the winds will blow in your favor if you have prepared yourself well for the task at hand.

You know, in many ways, you are like an artist. You are painting a picture of your life every day when you wake up. You will make mistakes as you move the brush, but you can always redraw and shade in a different color—life causes us to make adjustments along the way. This will not ruin your picture of life—in fact, it will make it more vibrant and captivating. It is up to you to paint the picture you want in the end. Don't let someone interfere with your artistic ability to draw your future. If I had allowed Sister Reparata (rest her soul) to define my picture of life, what would I have accomplished? Nothing! No, I was determined to prove her work, to develop my God-given talents, and to be the best I could be at whatever I chose to do! Thank you, Sister, you helped me define the Judy I became!

You can improve your life every day because you hold the pen in your hand that writes, corrects, or improves what you have done or are setting out to do. You should be the kind of person who looks for the road that will lead you to success and not the one who is always looking for excuses when things do not go your way.

I would also like to think that your life is like a stream of water. Once water has moved down the stream, it does not have the opportunity to come back because it can only flow forward. Follow the stream, take every ripple and ride them in to define who you are and what you are capable of achieving! Seize every opportunity before you, and prepare yourself to be the person that you were destined to become: a successful student who knows and who can do and who ultimately will be a pillar in their community.

I'll leave you again with my favorite quote: "Remember, you will walk this way but once, and you must make a difference, or your passing will have been in vain!"

Here's to your success. I'm so proud of you, but most importantly, you will be proud of yourself, and that is what matters!

ABOUT THE AUTHOR

Judy Loredo

Judith G. Loredo, Ph.D., is a pioneering Latina educator. In a career that spanned forty-nine years, she specialized in bridging the gap in public and postsecondary education, envisioning innovative pilot programs, and increasing opportunities for females and students of color. She is the twentieth recipient of the Dean Karl Brendt Award as the 1980 distinguished graduate of the College of Education at the University of Texas at Austin, holds three degrees from Our Lady of the Lake University, and holds a certificate of completion from San Antonio Junior College.

Dr. Loredo and her husband, Sonny, are the founders of Sembradores de Amistad (which means "sowers of friendship") Austin Chapter, a charitable foundation. Endowed scholarships for first-generation students have been established in Austin-area universities in the name of the organization. Among her long list of awards and recognitions are the Distinguished Woman Award from the Girl Scouts of Central Texas, Hispanic Chamber of Austin Education Leadership Award, National Hispanic Hall of Honor inductee, and Outstanding Professor Award from Sears, Roebuck, and Company. Additionally, she was named a Piper Professor at Huston-Tillotson University and was awarded professor emeritus status there. She and

Sonny, her husband of thirty-seven years, reside in Austin, Texas, as a blended family. Sonny and Judy have a total of six children, twenty-one grandchildren, and nine great-grandchildren. You can reach out to Dr. Loredo at failureturnedinsideout2020@gmail.com

Alex Montoya

Alex Montoya is an award-winning author, international speaker, and writing coach. As founder of A-Motivational Communications, he delivers inspirational keynote speeches and has published five books: *Swinging for the Fences (2008), The Finish Line (2012), See the Good (2016), Wolfpack* (2017), and *Living Inspired!: Motivating Your Kids, Colleagues, & Country (2018).* He also co-authored *Here Comes Cannonball!: Reflections on the 40th Anniversary of Anderson Plumbing, Heating & Air (2019).*

A graduate of the University of Notre Dame, with a master's degree from the University of San Francisco, he has spoken at Harvard, NASA, and Google. Alex is in the San Diego Unified School District Hall of Fame and was the featured author of the 2018 Literary Festival at Mira Costa College in Oceanside, California. He has also received a lifetime achievement award from the San Diego County Hispanic Chamber of Commerce and a medal of honor from the Colombian government. To learn more about his message of overcoming disabilities and other challenges, please visit www.alexmontoya.org. Montoya is a native of Medellin, Colombia, and resides in the San Diego, California, neighborhood of East Village.

Memories of Dr. Judith Ann Gutierrez Lozano Loredo

My mother, **Juliette Ramos Gutierrez**, was beautiful, kind, and inspiring. She was strong, too, who worked tirelessly to see that I would be educated to the fullest. She urged me to always to pursue my dreams. She devoted her life to helping me become the woman I am today. She passed way too soon!

Picture of my beloved father, Judge **Jaime P. Gutierrez**. My dad was an articulate, distinguished look who exuded confidence. He was a well-respected leader in the San Antonio Hispanic community. He always supported my dreams and encouraged me to be the best that I could be.

Picture with parents when attending a formal community event.

Picture of Judith as a young girl. Always dressed in frills and lace. Her grandmother always made her clothes.

I love dressing up and wearing evening attire. I represented the San Antonio Charro Association at the Feria De La Flores Gala and was selected Queen.

Debutant Ball Picture held in 1961 at the Granada Hotel in San Antonio Texas.

High school graduation from Providence High School, May 1964.

Graduation cap and gown picture from Our Lady of the Lake University—undergrad degree, Dec. 1968.

Graduation picture in doctoral robe from the University of Texas at Austin.

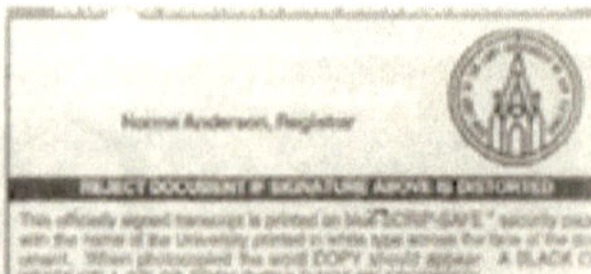

OLLU
OUR LADY OF THE LAKE UNIVERSITY

Norma Anderson, Registrar

REJECT DOCUMENT IF SIGNATURE ABOVE IS DISTORTED

Name of student

	Course No.	DESCRIPTION OF COURSE
		CREDITS FROM: SAN ANTONIO COLLEGE, SAN ANTONIO, TEXAS
PSY	301	Intro to Psychology
ENG	601A	English Composition
SPE	305	Fund of Speech
BIOL	601A	General Biology
SPAN	407	Inter Spanish
PE	101W	Physical Trng Women
SOC	102	Orientation
BIOL	651B	General Biology
ENG	601B	English Composition
HIST	615A	History of the US
PE	102W	Physical Trng Women
SPE	301	Voice & Diction
ENG	313	Read in World Lit
PE	111	Physical Trng Women
ENG	314	Read in World Lit
PE	112	Physical Trng Women
HIST	615B	History of the US
BIOL	601A	General Biology
GOVT	610A	American Government
ENG	601A	English Composition
SPAN	613A	Inter & Adv Comp & Conv
SPE	306	Public Speaking
GEOG	302	Geography
GOVT	610B	American Government
SPAN	612B	Inter & Adv Comp & Conv
SOC	301	Marriage and Family
PE	311	Health Educ Elem Sch
BIOL	601b	General Biology
		CREDITS FROM: OUR LADY OF THE LAKE COLLEGE, SAN ANTONIO, TEXAS
Spe	463	Psychopathology of Language
Ed	463	Survey of Exceptional Children
Psy	360	Psychology of Learning
Psy	630	Psychology of Personal Adjustment
Spe	375	Clinical Practice in Speech Correction

*Not counted toward degree. **Not transferrable. ***Only three semester

*Repeated course to raise grade.

(Continued on page 2)

OLLU
OUR LADY OF THE LAKE UNIVERSITY

Norma Anderson, Registrar

REJECT DOCUMENT IF SIGNATURE ABOVE IS DISTORTED

Name of student LOREDO (GUTIERREZ) JUDITH ANN

	Course No.	DESCRIPTION OF COURSE
Spe	475	Diagnostic Procedures in Speech
Spe	374	Speech and Language Habilitation of the Acoustically Handicapped Child
RelS	267	Marriage
Ed	492	Student Teaching in the Elementary School
Ed	493	Student Teaching in the Secondary School
Spe	463	Psychopathology of Language
RelS	360	Crisis of Faith
Ed	371	Curriculum & Instruction in the Elementary School
Spe	573	Fundamentals of Hearing and Hearing Testing
Psy	352	Social Psychology
Psy	370	Statistics for the Behavioral Sciences

BACHELOR OF ARTS DEGREE CONFERRED: DECEMBER 21, 1968
MAJOR: SPEECH PATHOLOGY   MINOR: PSYCHOLOGY

*Repeated course to raise grade.

OLLU
OUR LADY OF THE LAKE UNIVERSITY

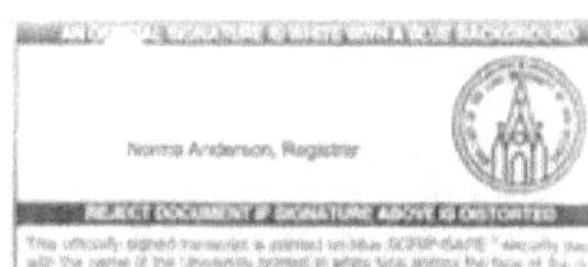
Norma Anderson, Registrar
REJECT DOCUMENT IF SIGNATURE ABOVE IS DISTORTED

OLLU
OUR LADY OF THE LAKE UNIVERSITY

THE UNIVERSITY OF TEXAS AT AUSTIN
OFFICE OF THE REGISTRAR, MAIN BLDG. ROOM 1, AUSTIN, TX 78712-1157, (512) 475-7575

FICE CODE: 3654   IPEDS CODE: 228778   ATP CODE: 6882   ACT CODE: 4240

OFFICIAL TRANSCRIPT

NAME: STUDENT ID: DATE: 01/23/06
                                                   DOB: PAGE: 1

DEGREES AWARDED BY THE UNIVERSITY OF TEXAS AT AUSTIN:

DEGREE: DOCTOR OF PHILOSOPHY
DATE: MAY 17, 1980
MAJOR: EDUCATIONAL ADMINISTRATION

ATTENDED: OUR LADY OF THE LAKE UNIVERSITY
          DEGREE AWARDED: B A   SPRING 1968
          DEGREE AWARDED: M A   SPRING 1972
          DEGREE AWARDED: M ED   SPRING 1975

          COURSEWORK UNDERTAKEN AT THE UNIVERSITY OF TEXAS AT AUSTIN

FALL SEMESTER 1976   GRADUATE SCHOOL
    EDA 388L SCHOOL LAW   3.0 A
HRS UNDERTAKEN 3   HRS PASSED 3   GPA HRS 3   GR PTS   12.00   GPA 4.0000

SPRING SEMESTER 1977   GRADUATE SCHOOL
    EDA 383   DESIGNING INSERVICE ED PROG   3.0 B
    EDA 388   LEADERSHIP THEORY & PRACTICE   3.0 CR
HRS UNDERTAKEN 6   HRS PASSED 6   GPA HRS 3   GR PTS   9.00   GPA 3.0000

FALL SEMESTER 1977   GRADUATE SCHOOL
    PSY 317   STAT METH PSYCH-SELF-PACED   3.0 B
    EDA 685   PRACTICUM IN PROGRAM DEVELOPMT   6.0 A
    EDA 395   PLANMAKING EDUC ENTERPRISES   3.0 B
    EDA 388   TOPICAL SEMINAR   3.0 CR
HRS UNDERTAKEN 15   HRS PASSED 12   GPA HRS 9   GR PTS   33.00   GPA 3.6666

SPRING SEMESTER 1978   GRADUATE SCHOOL
    MAN 380   PERSONNEL ADMINISTRATION PROBS   3.0 A
    EDA 383   RESEARCH METH-DATA ANALYSIS   3.0 A
    EDA 395   SUPERINTENDENCY MGT TEAM   3.0 A
    EDA 396   RESEARCH SEMINAR   3.0 A
    EDA 397P GRADUATE INTERNSHIP   3.0 A
HRS UNDERTAKEN 15   HRS PASSED 15   GPA HRS 15   GR PTS   60.00   GPA 4.0000

SUMMER SESSION 1978   GRADUATE SCHOOL
    B A S282S ADMINISTRATIVE ORGANIZATIONS   3.0 Q
    EDA F383 SUPERINTENDENCY COMPETENCIES   3.0 A
    EDA W388 TOPICAL SEMINAR   3.0 A
HRS UNDERTAKEN 6   HRS PASSED 6   GPA HRS 6   GR PTS   24.00   GPA 4.0000

FALL SEMESTER 1978   GRADUATE SCHOOL
    EDA 380L SCHOOL FINANCE   3.0 A
    EDA 382M ORGANIZ THEORY IN EDUCATION   3.0 A
    EDA 698R DISSERTATION   6.0 A
    ARC 380   PROGRAMMING   3.0 A
HRS UNDERTAKEN 15   HRS PASSED 9   GPA HRS 9   GR PTS   36.00   GPA 4.0000

                                                    MORE WORK ON NEXT PAGE

Shelby Stanfield, Registrar

This official transcript is printed on security paper and does not require a raised seal.

THE UNIVERSITY OF TEXAS AT AUSTIN
OFFICE OF THE REGISTRAR, MAIN BLDG. ROOM 1, AUSTIN, TX 78712-1157, (512) 475-7575

FICE CODE: 3658   IPEDS CODE: 228778   ATP CODE: 6882   ACT CODE: 4240

OFFICIAL TRANSCRIPT

NAME: STUDENT ID: DATE: 01/23/06
                                         DOB: PAGE: 2

```
SPRING SEMESTER 1979      GRADUATE SCHOOL.
    EDA  395   SUPERINTENDENCY MGT TEAM                     3.0   A
    EDA  395   SUPERINTENDENCY MGT TEAM                     3.0   A
    EDA  699W  DISSERTATION                                 6.0   *
HRS UNDERTAKEN 12   HRS PASSED 6    GPA HRS 6    GR PTS  24.00  GPA 4.0000

SUMMER SESSION 1979      GRADUATE SCHOOL.
    EDA  W699W  DISSERTATION                                6.0   *
HRS UNDERTAKEN 6    HRS PASSED 0    GPA HRS 0    GR PTS   0.00  GPA 0.0000

FALL SEMESTER 1979       GRADUATE SCHOOL.
    EDA  699W  DISSERTATION                                 6.0   *
HRS UNDERTAKEN 6    HRS PASSED 0    GPA HRS 0    GR PTS   0.00  GPA 0.0000

SPRING SEMESTER 1980     GRADUATE SCHOOL.
    EDA  399W  DISSERTATION                                 3.0   A
HRS UNDERTAKEN 3    HRS PASSED 0    GPA HRS 0    GR PTS   0.00  GPA 0.0000

        CUMULATIVE TOTALS EARNED AS A GRADUATE STUDENT AT U.T. AUSTIN
HRS UNDERTAKEN 87   HRS PASSED 57   GPA HRS 51   GR PTS  198.00  GPA 3.8823

           ***   END  OF  TRANSCRIPT  ***
```

This official transcript is printed on security paper and does not require a raised seal.

A sampling of my transcripts from Our Lady of the Lake University and the doctoral program at the University of Texas. Not bad for someone who was told by the nuns in high school I'd have to pay someone to let me graduate!

My husband, Sonny, is my rock and my strength!

Sonny and I have always believed in being leaders and giving back. We are attending a formal event in Capilla de Guadalupe, Mexico.

My biological children, Lloyd and Alysa. They grow up way too fast, but they are the light of my life!

My beautiful daughter, Alysa Denise, and adorable son, Lloyd Eleuterio.

A brilliant shot of my daughter, Alysa Denise, and her family: David Muto, son-in-law; Alessia Juliette Muto, granddaughter; Demetre Dominic Muto, grandson.

Sonny and I are a blended marriage. We both adore our kids, grandkids, and great-grandkids all year long, but the holidays are especially memorable for us.

My biological son, Lloyd L. Loredo, and his beautiful bride, Danielle Storey Loredo.

Wedding day for my son, Lloyd Eleuterio Loredo, who married the beautiful Danielle Storey. All my stepdaughters, with their husbands, and six of the grandchildren who participated in the wedding are pictured here.

My oldest stepdaughter, Virginia Loredo Gonzales; and her husband, Tony Gonzales; and their children, our grandchildren, Alexandria, Jacob, and Anthony. Very proud of these grandchildren—they are all college graduates!

Family picture of my second oldest stepdaughter, Dolores Loredo LeBlanc, at the wedding of her second daughter, Marianna LeBlanc, to Steven Longoria. Pictured is our son-in-law, Ret. Col. Joseph LeBlanc. Also pictured are their children, Joseph LeBlanc Jr.; Vincent LeBlanc and his wife, Jenny; Bro. Francis (Adam) LeBlanc; Anthony LeBlanc and his wife, Tracy; John Leblanc and his wife, Taylor; Jackie Mills and her husband, Caleb; Gabrielle Marie LeBlanc; and Benjamin LeBlanc, and their grandchildren.

Picture of my middle stepdaughter, Veronica Loredo Turman, and her family: Luke, our son-in law; Connor Thomas, our grandson, who will attend A&M University College of Engineering; and Ava Victoria, our granddaughter.

Photo of my youngest stepdaughter, Delisa Loredo Morris, and her family: Josh Morris, our son-in-law; Issac Morris; Maya Morris; Samuel Morris; Victoria Morris; and Maximillian Morris.

A great recognition came when the school cafeteria at St. Michael's Catholic Academy was named "in honor of Dr. Judith Loredo." This endeavor was funded by Jeff and Deanna Sera.

The building at St. Michael's Catholic Academy where Café Loredo is housed.

Prior to my marrying Sonny, this building—the Judith A. Lozano Professional Development Center—was named in my honor.

The Lozano Professional Development Center is located in the Southside Independent School District in historic San Antonio, Texas.

St. Gabriel's Catholic School in Austin, Texas, where I was a founding member of the board of directors.

Fifteen years ago Judith Ann Gutierrez Lozano had only one ambition in life — to fulfill her parents' dream of her completing college.

Having graduated in the top 25 percent of her class high school class at the age of 16, choosing a career would be no problem for her.

Today, the 33-year-old native San Antonian is superintendent of the Southside Independent School District, the first woman school superintendent in Bexar County and the only Mexican-American woman superintendent in Texas. She is also the youngest to hold that position. Her plans are to make the district one of the best.

"The district has every possibility of becoming one of the outstanding school districts in the state," she said.

Although she graduated among the top of her class at Providence High School in 1964, she was not sure of what career to choose. Helping the handicapped has always been part of her. It was in the middle of her first year at San Antonio College that she became interested in communication disorders.

"I knew then I did not want to be a regular school teacher," she said. "I wanted to become more involved in speech therapy centers."

Medicine

There was a time, however, when she was interested in medicine. She thought of becoming a neurosurgeon. The functions of the brain interested her. "But I never thought I had the ability to graduate from medical school."

She obtained her certification of completion from SAC in 1966 and enrolled at Our Lady of the Lake University where she obtained her bachelor of arts degree in communication disorders. The educator recalled her commitment to fulfilling her parents' dream of her graduating from college.

Somehow, however, simply getting a bachelor's degree was not enough. She embarked on a long and often difficult road and obtained two master's degrees and a doctorate.

In 1970, while working on her first masters' degree, she became a speech therapist for the Edgewood School District, where she provided speech and language services to about 180 students located on four elementary campuses. This included administering hearing, speech and language evaluations; writing up diagnostic reports; developing speech and language educational plans; consulting with parents and teachers; and presenting speech and language development workshops.

served as a consultant in the Division of Compensatory Education for TEA.

She obtained her Ph.D. in educational administration. Judy was recipient of the 1980 Dean Karl Brett Award as a distinguished graduate of the College of

When I became the first female superintendent in Texas, it was literally headline news!

Article when I was honored by the Central Texas Girl Scouts at their annual Women of Distinction Luncheon.

CON MI MADRE AWARD: DR. JUDITH LOREDO

Presented to an educated successful Latina who is living out our mission and serves as a role model for the young Latinas and mothers in our program.

Dr. Loredo holds a Certificate of Completion from San Antonio College; a BS in the Science of Communication Disorders, an MA in Speech Pathology, and a M.ED. in Education, from Our Lady of the Lake University; and a Ph.D from the University of Texas at Austin.

Dr. Loredo has a career spanning more than 48 years in the field of education. She has been a speech pathologist, a teacher, a Director of Early Childhood Education, the Superintendent of Schools of Southside Independent School District in San Antonio, Texas, the Assistant to the Deputy Commissioner for Programs & Administration at Texas Education Agency, the Dean of Academic Affairs at Huston-Tillotson University, the Assistant Commissioner for the Division of P-16 Education, Texas Higher Education Coordinating Board and everything in between. Dr. Loredo retired in 2014, only to come out of retirement moments later to serve as the Coordinator of MSI-TEN LBJ Institute for STEM Education & Research/EPDC - NASA Grant, Texas State University.

Dr. Loredo has been the recipient of many awards throughout her career, far too many to list them all. The following are a sampling of her many accomplishments: Distinguished Professor, Joe & Theresa Long Legacy Award awarded by UT Austin Division of Diversity; Woman of Distinction, Central Texas Girl Scouts Association; Hispanic Chamber of Commerce Education Leadership Award; Outstanding Leader in Education, Greater Austin Hispanic Chamber of Commerce; and the Joseph T. McMillan Endowed Professor in Teacher Education. In addition, Dr. Loredo holds the distinction of being the first Hispanic female elected to the position of Superintendent of Schools in Texas.

Dr. Loredo has served on numerous Boards including but not limited to the Civil Service Commission City of Austin/Vice-Chair; Mayor's Women Commission; Greater Austin Hispanic Chamber Foundation Board/Vice-Chair; 8212 Women's Auxiliary of Barton Creek Country Club, Con Mi MADRE; Founding Board Member St. Gabriel's Catholic School, Past Board Member St. Michael's Catholic Academy where the Cafeteria was named in her honor.

In her spare time, Dr. Loredo and her husband, Sonny Loredo have created a blended family - together they have five daughter's; one son, twenty-one grandchildren and six great grand-children.

Receiving this award touched me right in the heart. It is the Corazon Award given annually to a deserving individual who has contributed up and beyond to the Con Mi MADRE Program, a 501c3 nonprofit organization in Austin, Texas.

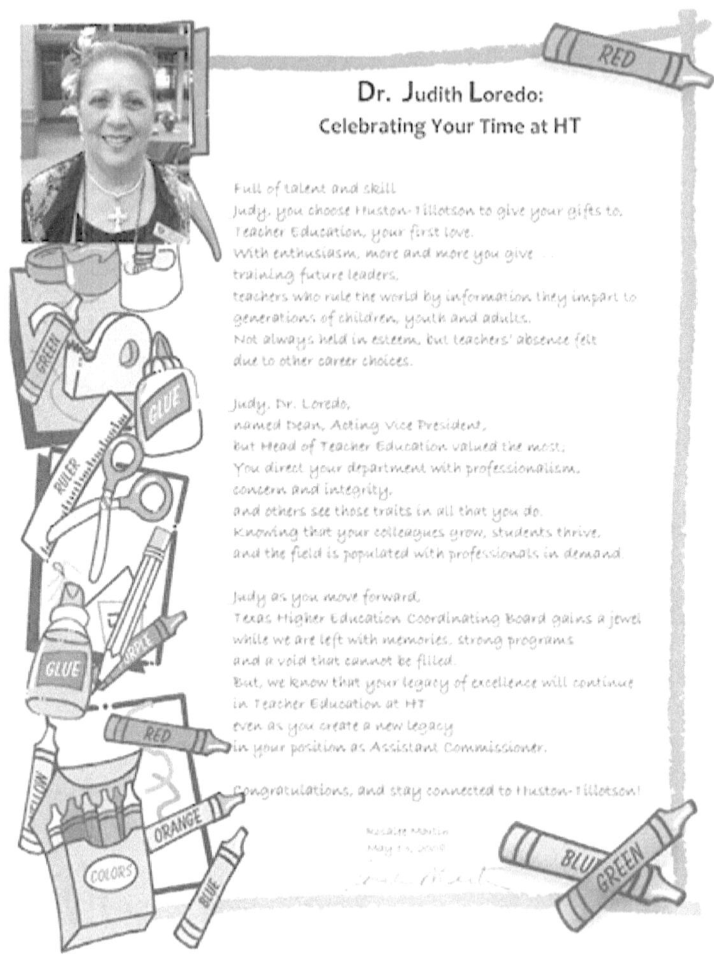

Huston-Tillotson brought me to tears with these words of thanks when I left the institution after twenty-two years.

TO YOU MY FRIEND ON THIS OUR DAY....
MOTHER'S DAY

*In the busiest of times, in frightening times, in the saddest
of times, and in the happiest of times – I think of you! I
think of you more so on this our Special Day.... Mother's Day.*

*Why do I think of you today? Because I think of all the
beautiful qualities that you possess as a Mother, a friend,
a confidant, and as a Woman!*

*The flowers on this paper are sent to you to thank you for all you do.
I am also asking God
To watch over you – to keep you healthy, and free from harm today and
Everyday because this world would be empty without your presence as a
Mother, as my friend and as a Woman!*

*Have you ever stopped to think how many lives you affect daily?
Your spouse, significant other, your children, you're extended family,
Your friends, your church family, your neighbors, your colleagues at work,
the employees where you shop, the stranger on the street. To each
of these and many more you are special today because you are
someone's Mother, Step-mother, Grandmother, Surrogate Mother,
Adopted Mother, God-Mother or that special someone who is "like a mother".*

*You may not carry a professional title, you may not have fame, and you may not
have received awards, nor have written a book, you may not have a vita
pages long, or have prestige to carry you along! You may not be thin or beautiful,
tall, rich or traveled, but you are that special person - someone calls Mother!*

*You are more beautiful and you have greater fame with a richness that money
Cannot buy –Because you have shouldered someone's pain; you have wiped
Someone's tear; you have healed someone's hurt; you have laughed, cried and
cheered for those you love. You have asked "what can I do?" and expected
nothing in return!*

*Not too many can do the things you do and continue to do, because it takes a special
Someone like you – So on this your Day it is no doubt why I should ask the Angles to
watch over you, because you are special and you wear so many hats.*

*Remembering you today in spite of distance or circumstance – because you are
My Special Friend! Thank you for being the Mother that you are but most
of all - Thank you for being My Friend!*

Happy Mother's Day

Love............Dr. Judith Loredo

A special Mother's Day poem that I wrote. I write a Mother's Day poem every year and send it out to about two hundred women whose friendship means a great deal to me!

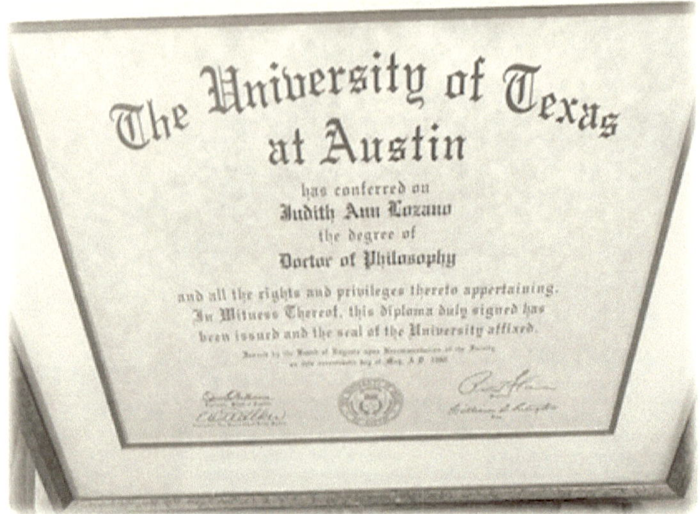

My doctoral degree from the University of Texas.

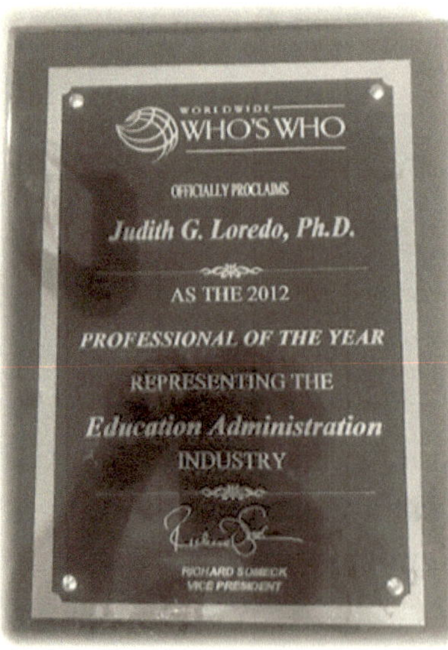

Cambridge Who's Who! Can you believe it?

Overwhelmed with pride when the Hall of Honor included me.

A great recognition from the University of Texas at Austin!

Thank you, United Way!

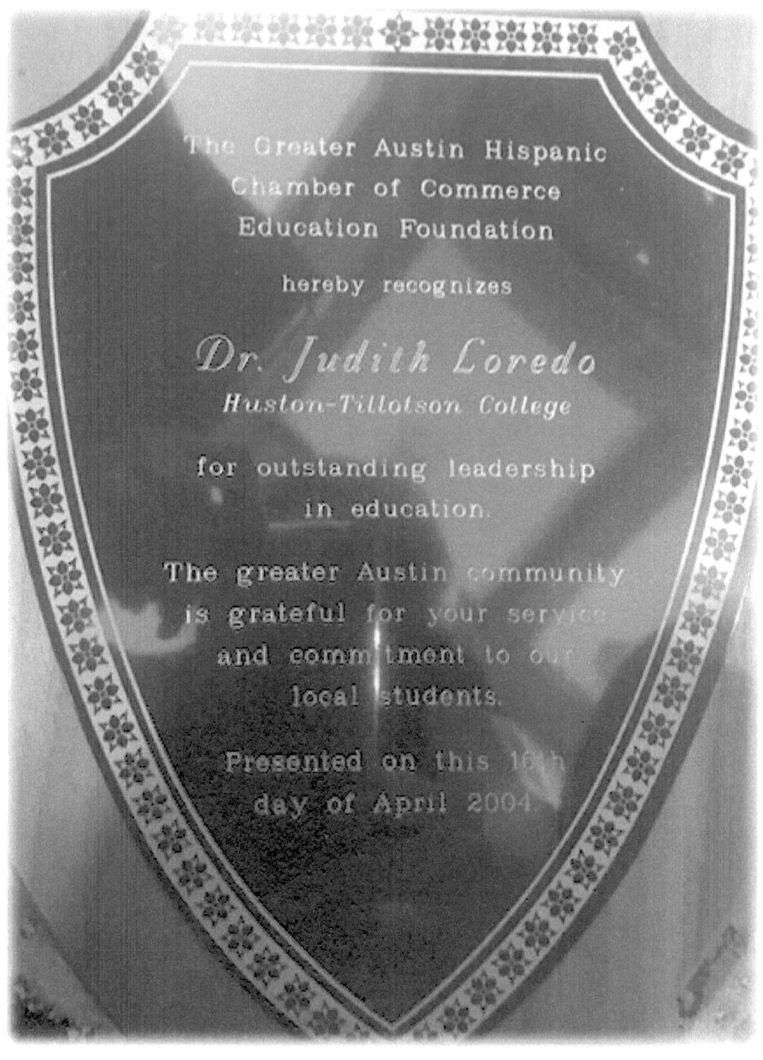

Thrilled by this award from the Greater Austin Hispanic Chamber of Commerce Education Foundation.

St. Michael's Catholic Academy in Austin has such a special place in my heart.

What They're Saying about Judy

Dr. Loredo's story is a fascinating personal journey of resilience that will give the reader inspiration to work through their own challenges in life and become the best they can be. She has been my mentor and exemplar for years. This book acts as a mentor for Latinas everywhere who may be in school, parenting, teaching, or leading organizations. *¡Que inspiración!*
   —Melissa M. Chavez, PhD

   Associate Vice President and Superintendent,
   The University of Texas Charter School
   System/Division of Diversity & Community Engagement
   The University of Texas at Austin

Dr. Loredo's encouragement set a course for my life that allowed me to become all that God had created for me. She became my mentor and friend. As I moved from adjunct instructor to department chair to associate provost, she was the individual I looked to for counsel and advice. She is an exceptional educator and a wonderful person. I am blessed to have such a person guiding me through my professional endeavors.
   —Dr. Eric Budd

   Chair, Department of Education
   Huston-Tillotson University

Dr. Loredo is one of the kindest and most compassionate persons I know. I had the privilege of working with her at the Texas Higher Education Coordinating Board for 11 years. It wasn't until several years after working together that I became aware of her learning disability and how she independently overcame it and other obstacles. She is a positive role model, particularly for low-income Latinas who struggle academically. Her success story reveals how true grit—or as we say in Spanish, ganas— plays a critical role in helping students achieve their lifelong goals.

—Linda Battles, MPAff

Deputy Commissioner for Agency Operations and Communications/COO
Texas Higher Education Coordinating Board

Without a doubt, the Texas Higher Education Coordinating Board was the most demanding job of my career. The executive leadership team was 10–12 people charged with coordinating higher education in Texas. Not an easy task, but Judy was welcoming as a colleague and friend. I could sense how compassionate she was about helping students implement the best state policy for students. I think her entire career is reflective of this love for students.

—Garry Tomerlin, EdD

Government Relations & Strategic Initiatives Tech-Labs Inc.

Dr. Loredo served as our superintendent of schools during my tenure as a board member. The majority of our students were Hispanic and economically deprived. But she was able to increase the academic performance throughout the district and had good relationships with the district patrons and school staff.

—David S. Smith

Former Board of Directors member Southside School District

Dr. Judy Loredo is a champion for students of color. As motivation for her pupils, Dr. Loredo shared her own difficulties as a student to illustrate the value of positive thinking and determination. These accounts of her educational challenges highlight her resolve to obtain an education in ways in which she utilized obstacles as opportunities to overcome what her teachers saw as impediments to her ability to achieve.

This book demystifies the path to higher education and college success. It is a must-read for students of color, their parents, school counselors, recruitment and retention committees, and college admissions staff.
—Alicia Moore,

Endowed Professor
Southwestern University (Georgetown, TX)

Dr. Judy Loredo is a pioneer among higher education leaders and an inspiration to so many. Her story of resilience and triumph is a testament to the potential of all our students, regardless of what obstacles they have to navigate or overcome. Dr. Loredo's legacy lives on in the countless individuals that she mentored and inspired throughout her illustrious career, including many from underrepresented backgrounds.
—Victor B. Sáenz, PhD

Chair and Professor, Department of Educational
Leadership and Policy
Executive Director, Project MALES and Texas Education
Consortium for Male Students of Color
The University of Texas at Austin

Dr. Loredo is a great example of extraordinary commitment to higher education.

—Larry L. Earvin, PhD

Chief of Staff, Southern Association of Colleges and Schools Commission on Colleges (SACSCOC)

Dr. Loredo has been an outstanding educational leader in Texas for more than 40 years. I first met her as she pursued doctoral studies in 1977 and have closely followed her highly successful career since that date. She served both as a Texas public school superintendent as well as a college professor at Huston-Tillotson University.

While she championed the education of all children, she chose to work in particularly challenging areas with concentrations of poor and minority students. She believes that all children can learn and that it is the obligation of educators to find ways to help all students reach their potentials and dreams. I am pleased to commend this book of her story of overcoming obstacles and challenges as an inspirational account of the rewards of hard work, dedication, and diligence.

—William N. Kirby, PhD

Texas Commissioner of Education, 1984–1991

Dr. Judith Loredo: Administrator, Educator, Teacher

An excellent administrator, educator, and teacher is honest, has integrity, and is knowledgeable.

Dr. Judith (Judy) Loredo is an excellent administrator and teacher. When I moved to Austin, Texas in 2000 to become vice president for academic and student affairs, Dr. Judith Loredo, the chair of the education department, was the first academic leader to assure me of their support.

In our first conversations, she exuded a spirit of collegiality and a willingness to collaborate with me and others to achieve academic excellence for Huston- Tillotson College. Her commitment to the mission and goals of the college were paramount in her decision-making. The qualities of collaboration, collegiality, and commitment were the fundamental attributes that Judy demonstrated and were the reasons I chose her to become the academic dean for the college.

Dr. Judith Loredo became my most trusted colleague and friend in Austin, Texas. Her creative, compassionate, and visionary leadership, her scholarship, and her travels were the assets that shaped her understanding of people and power. With competence and kindness, Judy led the academic programs and developed new initiatives to assist us to graduate students who could meet the local, state, and national student learning outcomes and contribute effectively in their professions. She achieved these tasks always with a flourish for style and an engaging smile.

Dr. Judith Loredo became my friend. I could trust her; I could depend on her—her loyalty was never a question. Judy welcomed me into her life. Judy was my bridge to all things Austin, Texas. Judy was my confidante during difficult days, and she remains my trusted friend.

    —Sandra Chambers Vaughn, PhD
    Rust College
    Professor of Political Science (Ret.)
    Vice President for Academic Affairs
    SACSCOC Liaison

I am lucky to call Dr. Loredo my mother and one of my mentors. Throughout my entire life, Mom has always pushed me to continue my education, which embodies what she has done for so many other people and organizations throughout her life. My mom is a true testament to what hard work and determination can produce. I will never forget the first time that my mom told me about a teacher she had who told her she would never amount to anything, but through the grace of God and her determination, she proved that teacher wrong. I will never forget the amount of math and science books that my mom would bring on vacation so that when we had downtime, I could continue to learn. My mom is the reason that I have a master's in accounting. I talk to my mom every day to say hello but sometimes to ask her advice, and I am grateful that no matter what time of day, she is always there to speak with me. I would not be the person that I am if it were not for my mom.

Mom—I love you and thank you for your continual guidance throughout life.
—Lloyd Eleuterio Loredo, MSA

VP, Loredo Truss Company Inc.
Austin, Texas

My mom in a word ... *motivational.* I don't think my mom set out to teach me anything in life—she showed me! Always pushing me to be the very best version of me that I could be.

This book is an exceptional read of a collection of the stories of my mother's life and the many challenges she faced in life that led her to be the very well-known "Dr. Loredo." Her educational passion shines through in this book. It will not only inspire but it will challenge its readers. There's no doubt it will make a difference in the lives of women. Even knowing my mother, my best friend, as well as I do, I was still so deeply moved by her book.

All that I am or ever hope to be, I owe to my mom!
—Alysa D. Muto

Daughter of Dr. Judith Loredo
Chief Operating Officer
Hospital Internists of Texas
Austin, Texas

The dirt parking lot was likely muddy that morning, as it was most days. The day before, the director of special education for the Edgewood Independent School District had been fired. The year was 1975, and I was a year into the job. I sat in a portable classroom at the end of Castroville Road with my special education colleagues, awaiting her replacement who would be our new supervisor. I remember Larry Rourke, immaculately dressed, always hiking up his pants and laughing while nervously jiggling his large frame; Marina Serbantez, a soft-spoken former nun from San Benito, Texas; Jose Leyva, beautiful Debbie Schumacher with short blond hair; Barbara Schmitt; and maybe, Barbara Eisenhower was there. The others in the room are but shadows.

While we awaited the arrival of the new director, we conjured up images of what she might be like. It would be Bessie Bryant, an older African American female, a rarity in those days and especially in southwestern San Antonio, that would break the awkward silence by saying, "Be careful how you treat people on the way up because you'll never know who you'll meet on the way down". My transformation into professional dress came early in our first meeting when I was chastised for my too casual Western Levi's, dress shirt, and tie. Lesson learned: it would be a suit after that.

Judy was grace and compassion—traits learned from her mother, the model of an elegant Hispanic woman. Her self-discipline, tenacity, and insight would come from her father, an esteemed San Antonio judge. Judy's unwavering moral compass—a gift from both of her parents. An only child of older parents, no one ever told her that she *should* not do something—and she learned early on that there was nothing that she *could* not do. Family has always been her center. Her love and compassion for others melded from her varied roles of wife, mother, daughter, and career educator.

In 1975, the Edgewood Independent School District was the second poorest school district in the state of Texas. The implementation model for the education of exceptional children was Plan A—the forerunner of PL 94-142 (the national law identifying and requiring identified children with special needs, ages 3–21 to be served by local school districts and local educational agencies across the states), and Child Find (a statewide effort to locate previously unidentified and unserved children). Child Find found few children. The districts generally already knew that these invisible children existed at the end of some dusty road in a blue battered trailer but simply chose not to identify them because to do so would require them to then expend scarce funds and subsequently serve them, "in the least restrictive environment."

It was against this backdrop that I met Judy Loredo. I had been hired as a liaison between the school district and the San Antonio Children's Center (SACC), a free- standing child psychiatric facility. My task was to create a self-contained elementary and middle school class of seriously emotionally disturbed children and youth identified by district campuses and to establish a continuum of mental health services that allowed some children who were too disturbed for an outpatient self- contained school setting to be admitted into SACC. The model minimized the frequency of inpatient state hospitalization for severely emotionally disturbed children and extended mental health consultation to local school district principals and administration and families for the first time. Plan A was visionary and, because Texas was on the 'cutting edge' of program innovation, came to serve as a template for PL 94-142. It is noteworthy that California, known as a leader in public education in the nation at that time, did not see a similar school-based implementation model for emotionally disturbed children and adolescents for the next twenty years.

In 1977, Judy left Edgewood to pursue her doctoral degree at the University of Texas at Austin, commuting home on weekends to her husband and daughter, Alyssa. After her departure, I left for Indiana University to pursue my doctoral degree, becoming a licensed psychologist in California in 1988.

As I write this, I realize that Judy's influence on me and my professional track began with that first meeting on Castroville Road. I learned my own management skills from her as I watched her surround herself with others that complemented her own tool kit. She led by example; professional jealousy was absent. Judy's scope of influence was extensive. As a special education director for the Edgewood Independent School District, she was the lone female among a group of mostly Latino male administrators and principals. Her presence as an articulate, attractive, and assertive female was a threat to many elementary and secondary principals who had created their fiefdoms based on self-interest throughout years of stagnation and bureaucracy in the district.

Judy was a tireless advocate for the poor and disenfranchised. Through the years, I have come to realize that the professional leadership that Judy modeled and the opportunities that she provided me have guided my career path, and countless lives have been indirectly impacted by her mentorship through the years. That southwestern area of San Antonio demographically housed active or former migrant farmworkers who formed the migration stream through the middle states of the United States and who returned to Edgewood and South Texas during the winter months. Migrant farmworkers generally died in their early forties because of prolonged exposure to pesticides and farm-related accidents. Only seven of one hundred migrant children entering high school would ultimately graduate because of differing accreditation standards between states, as their families lived their migratory lifestyle. It was a snapshot in time—and little has changed except the addition of portable toilets in the strawberry fields along State Road 126 near me now in Oxnard, California.

It would be Swiss psychoanalyst, Carl Jung, who would coin the term "synchronicity," or "accidental coincidences." It is not, however, an accident that forty- five years later, the same woman that would chastise me for wearing Levi's to work would become a professional colleague and, most importantly, a lifelong friend.

—David Joel Jimenez, EdD
California Psychology Lic. No. PSY10629

Judith Ann Loredo, PhD

Profile

- Over thirty years of experience in higher education administration and teaching
- Doctor of Philosophy in Educational Administration
- Professor emerita (2008) at Huston-Tillotson University (HTU)
- Proven student-focused leader, fundraiser, financial and strategic planner
- Excellent communication and motivational skills
- Served as board member/trustee for over twenty-three years in academic, business, government, and nonprofit organizations in Austin and San Antonio
- Traveled extensively abroad—Mexico, Central America, South America, Africa, Alaska, Russia, China, Caribbean
- English-Spanish bilingual

Career Positions Held

- Speech therapist, Edgewood Independent School District
- Director of special education, Edgewood Independent School District
- Superintendency fellow in the UT Austin Educational Administration Program
- Internship assignment as the assistant to the assistant commissioner for Professional Development at the Texas Education Agency

- Internship assignment as the assistant to the deputy commissioner at the Texas Education Agency
- Consultant in the Division of Compensatory Education, Texas Education Agency
- Superintendent of schools, Southside ISD in San Antonio, Texas
- Assistant to the director of the Superintendent Training Program, UT Austin
- Chairperson, Department of Education, Huston-Tillotson College, Austin, Texas
- Dean of Academic Affairs, Huston-Tillotson College, Austin, Texas
- Dean of Academic Support Program, Huston-Tillotson University, Austin, Texas
- Assistant Commission Division of P-16 Initiatives, Texas Higher Education Coordinating Board, Austin, Texas
- Assistant to the director of the NASA Project funded awarded to Texas State University, College of Education, overseeing and coordinating services of Colleges awarded grants in the Project

Major Honors

- Selected as first woman superintendent of schools in Texas, Southside ISD

- Selected as Outstanding Community Leader in Education by the San Antonio Newspaper

- Having a building named in her honor by the Southside ISD Board of Trustees—the Dr. Judith Lozano Assessment Center for Teaching Excellence

- Presidential Award for Teaching Excellence, HTU

- Sears-Roebuck Teaching Excellence Award

Minnie Piper Professor Award for Teaching Excellence

- Twentieth recipient of the Dean Carl Brendt Award as a distinguished graduate of the College of Education, UT, Austin (Piper and this award are two different awards by different organizations. Dean Carl Brendt is from UT Austin College of Education and Piper Professor Award is out of San Antonio Texas Piper Foundation)
- Selected as Woman of Distinction by the Girls Scouts of Central Texas
- Who's Who Publishers presents "Top 101 Industry Experts – Insights and Ideas to Inspire You" 2014 ISBN:978-1-60758-680-7
- Honored by the Hispanic Chamber of Commerce Foundation Board for Outstanding Leadership in Education
- Cafeteria named in her honor by the board of trustees—Café Loredo at St. Michael's Catholic Academy in Austin, Texas; funds provided by Jeff and Deanna Sera

- Inducted by the Hispanic Sports Foundation for Education Inc. into the National Hispanic Heritage Hall of Honor
- Listed in Cambridge Who's Who Registry of Executives, Professionals and Entrepreneurs Listed in worldwide Who's Who in the Educational Administration Industry

Professional Achievements

- Developed responses to approximately nineteen recommendations cited by the Southern Association of Colleges and Schools (SACS) for academic program accreditation deficiencies that resulted in full SACS accreditation.
- Facilitated total redesign of HTU Teacher Education Program offerings in both elementary and secondary education that led to full accreditation by the Texas Education Agency (TEA).
- Developed documentation for HTU to implement an alternative teacher certification program that received TEA approval for EC-6, secondary and all-level certification programs.
- Developed and implemented HTU criminal justice degree program that received SACS accreditation approval. The criminal justice degree program was part of the first adult degree program evening class offerings.
- Prepared and submitted nomination forms leading to HTU being named as a finalist for the Texas Higher Education Coordinating Board (THECB)

Star Award for demonstrating excellence in teacher education preparation after exceeding the state standard of performance.

- Served as HTU dean of academic affairs, overseeing monthly faculty meetings, new curricula development, program evaluations, and supervision of over forty faculty members.
- Assisted in the development and implementation of semester course schedules for all academic majors for over four years.
- Developed partnership with the University of Texas at Austin bookstore for the purchase and packaging of textbooks to enhance academic performance for HTU freshman students.
- Prepared presentations and disseminated materials for HTU Board of Trustee quarterly meetings.
- Facilitated the planning and implementation of major HTU annual activities, including Charter Day, Honors Convocation, and graduation.
- Supervised the development and implementation of an assessment counseling process for monitoring performance of students admitted on academic or scholastic probation. In addition, a Texas higher education assessment (THEA) and diagnostic placement test was implemented for students seeking admission.
- Facilitated the development of a new statewide THECB Texas success initiative assessment, including a diagnostic component for determining college readiness that was implemented by Texas colleges and universities in the fall of 2013.

- Oversaw THECB development of postsecondary advancement via individual determination (AVID) program implemented at seventeen campuses across the state for the purpose of increasing the success of at-risk students entering postsecondary education.
- Managed college readiness legislative annual budget in excess of thirty-three million dollars for each biennial from 2008 to 2014.
- Supervised over twenty-six staff overseeing more than thirty statewide programs for the Division of P-16 Initiatives, now known as the Division of College Readiness and Success, at the THECB.
- Participated in development through proposed policies for legislative consideration and rules addressing mandated legislation in the area of college readiness, student success, and education preparation for the THECB affecting sixty-five Texas community colleges and thirty-six Texas colleges and universities.
- Served as THECB representative for State Board of Educational Certification and Accelerate Texas state projects.
- Addressed House Bill 44, the statewide redesign of developmental education, by overseeing the development and implementation of all activities related to improving education and outcomes for students in need of remedial education, including the development of adult basic education services.
- Provided academic advising and development of course semester schedule plans for an average of 75–150 students on scholastic probation.

- Served as administrative representative in executive cabinet meetings, both at the university level and as part of board meetings and board committee meetings at the state level.
- Facilitated the development and implementation of the HTU revised college bulletin every two years while serving as dean of academic affairs over a four-year period.
- Assisted in the development and implementation of the Center for Accelerated Learning, a student-tutoring center that provided tutors for students identified as in need of academic assistance at HTU.
- Oversaw the development and implementation of the infrastructure of total internet access across the HTU campus.
- Served as president of the Deans of Teacher Certification Organization for the Consortium of State Organizations for Texas Teacher Education and participated in state-level teacher education committees.
- Served as chair of the Certification Advisory Committee for the State Department of Higher Education that coordinated the recommendation of program offerings at colleges and universities.
- Guided the statewide redesign for development education in response to a legislative mandate. At present, all colleges and universities across the state are implementing the revised program.
- Guided and monitored the implementation of statewide adult basic education initiatives in Texas community colleges.

- Guided the development and implementation of the new Texas Success Initiatives Assessment test for determining college readiness, which, for the first time, includes a diagnostic component for academic placement.
- Developed and guided the implementation of program initiatives that speak to closing the gap for minority males to increase participation and completion for African American and Latino males.
- Monitored the implementation of the College and Career Readiness Standards in the K–12 curriculum statewide.
- Guided the implementation of college readiness activities designed to align K–12 and postsecondary curriculum.
- Guided the development and implementation of the College Readiness Student Success Initiative in over seventeen colleges statewide to decrease the drop-out rate of students in entry level college courses.
- Guided the development and implementation of statewide initiatives related to science, technology, engineering, and math (STEM) teacher training at three universities.
- Monitored the implementation of the federally funded Teacher Quality Partnership Grant that provides training for in-service teachers in the areas of math and science education, with approximately three to five million in grant funding.

- Guided the state effort in the redesign of teacher training using the teacher residency model in a collaboration with two universities.
- Participated in the state's development of the state strategic plan to focus on workforce education in postsecondary education approved by the THECB in July 2015.
- Served as the THECB representative to the State Board for Educator Certification.
- Oversaw the development and implementation of all activities related to improving the performance of students in need of remedial education, including the testing center, at HTU.
- Advised and counseled all students not meeting college readiness standards who were entering Huston-Tillotson University.
- Advised all HTU students on scholastic probation each semester in the course schedule preparation while serving as head of academic support.
- Guided the process for placing and monitoring HTU students on academic suspension.
- Worked closely with the office of the provost for academic and student affairs at HTU in all matters related to improving student performance and retention.
- Worked closely with the dean of arts and sciences at HTU to develop course schedules and all duties as assigned.
- Participated in all executive cabinet meetings at HTU.

- Participated in the development and implementation of all university-sponsored events related to student recruitment and registration.
- Convened all subcommittees related to academic programs at Huston-Tillotson University.
- Guided the process for addressing the academic violations and probation status of Huston-Tillotson University related to its reaccreditation process. Based on proposed and implemented revisions, the Southern Association of Colleges and Schools gave full accreditation to HTU in 2002.
- Developed and implemented agendas for the P-16 division subcommittee of the Texas Higher Education Coordinating Board.
- Guided the development and implementation of the student-tutoring center (Center for Student Acceleration) at HTU.
- Initiated the development and later implementation of the common course numbering system used by public colleges and universities in the course numbers of HTU course offerings to ease the process for students transferring into or out of HTU.
- Participated in all convocations at HTU and guided the process while serving as dean of academic affairs.
- Participated in all cabinet-level meetings at HTU.
- Participated and represented HTU when called upon to serve on THEB committees.
- Worked closely with HTU faculty when they needed assistance with students at risk of failing.

- Taught courses in the Department of Teacher Education at HTU.
- Worked on the redesign and implementation of the HTU Freshman Orientation Course.
- Taught sections of the Freshman Orientation Course, including a seminar for all freshmen entitled "This Isn't High School."
- Served as chair/dean of the Department of Teacher Education at HTU while also serving as dean of academic and student support services.
- Facilitated the development and redesign of the teacher preparation and the kinesiology programs at HTU to include changes required by the state.
- Implemented and improved programmatic activities in the HTU Division of Education that resulted in full accreditation in teacher education
- Guided the development and implementation of HTU online offerings in teacher education.
- Guided the development and implementation of the infrastructure for HTU campus-wide internet access, including a distance learning platform.
- Developed documents required for the TEA approval process for HTU to implement the Alternative Teacher Certification Program.
- Advised all students seeking teacher certification at HTU.
- Developed all semester schedules for the Department of Teacher Education and Kinesiology at HTU.
- Developed and monitored all budgets for both internal and external funding from the THECB and

the Sid Richardson Foundation for HTU teacher education and kinesiology programs.

Strategic Planning

- Supervised documentation, processes, and committees related to the development of the Huston-Tillotson University 2005–2010 Strategic Plan.
- Managed the implementation of the statewide closing-the-gap plan for six years, which THECB developed to address the goal for the number of students to be admitted into postsecondary education and increase the number of African American and Latino males in Texas higher education.
- Oversaw the state implementation of the College Access Challenge Grant as designated by the Texas governor's office. The multimillion-dollar grant provided funding to increase the number of students entering and completing postsecondary education in Texas.

Development/Fundraising

- Founded with husband, Eleuterio "Sonny" Loredo, the Austin Chapter of the Sembradores de Amistad, raising over $700,000 to create four endowed scholarships for first-generation students at area colleges and universities: Huston-Tillotson University, Concordia Lutheran University, the

University of Texas at Austin, and St. Edward's University.

- Served on more than twenty-three community boards and nonprofit organizations, in either a leadership or development capacity, for the purpose of raising funds for specifically targeted results. Fundraising was a requirement of all board memberships. Participation included chairing or cochairing fundraising events for the organization.

Former Board Memberships

- Board member, Wonders & Worries
- Executive board member, 8212 Women's Auxiliary, Barton Creek Country Club—positions serviced in: president-elect, president, parliamentarian, and hospitality chair (current)
- Advisory board member, Women of Distinction Advisory
- Board and Central Texas Girl Scouts
- Board member, Laguna Gloria Art Museum
- Board member, Brackenridge Hospital
- Board member, Austin Children's Museum
- Board member, Safe Place
- Board member, United Way of Austin Advisory
- Board (representing Huston-Tillotson University)
- Founding board member, St Gabriel's Catholic School
- Founding board member and president, Club Sembradores de San Antonio
- Founding board member, Club Sembradores de Austin

- Member and chair, Austin Commission for Women
- Member and vice chair, Civil Service Commission of Austin
- Member and chair, Catholic Diocese of Austin School Board
- Member and regional chair, Austin Lyric Opera Advisory Board
- Member, advisory board, Junior League of Austin
- Member, advisory board, Central Texas Girl Scouts
- Member, board of trustees, St. Michael's Catholic Academy
- Secretary, vice chair, and chair, Academic Committee, St. Michael's Catholic Academy
- Member, board of directors, Con Mi MADRE of Austin

Current Board Membership

- Chairperson, Greater Austin Hispanic Chamber of Commerce Foundation Board
- Member, Settlement Home Inc. (served as chair of its quinceañera celebration)

Collaboration

- Utilized funds provided through legislative mandate and managed the total redesign for online learning that connected Texas's five historically black colleges with a distance learning platform.
- Responded to legislative mandate by facilitating the state's design for developmental education that has presently been implemented by more than sixty-eight Texas colleges and universities.

- Oversaw the implementation of the state's adult basic education statewide initiative, including professional training begun in fall 2015.
- Assisted with the development and implementation of three higher education bridging programs developed to serve students in grades 11 and 12 and provide first-year persistence programs for first-year students dropping out of college and developmental education for recent high school graduates not ready for college.
- Supervised and assisted with the development of the Texas Comprehensive Student Success Program that aimed to improve student success in postsecondary education by providing a comprehensive program of interventions to increase completion of either a diploma or certification program. Targeted student populations are first-generation college students, with an emphasis on underrepresented student groups such as African American, Hispanic, or economically disadvantaged students. Five institutions of higher education have been involved in the implementation of this program: Austin Community College, Central Texas College, Houston Community College System, North Central Texas College, and the University of Houston–Downtown.
- Oversaw the development and implementation of the Texas Pathways Project, creating local partnerships between secondary and postsecondary institutions in a common pattern (e.g., multiple districts, local community colleges,

and the regional four-year institution that draws a significant number of students from the other partners). The program is designed to improve secondary to postsecondary transition and success through data-informed decisions. Institutions involved in the development of the program included Alamo Colleges, Houston Community College System, San Jacinto College District, South Texas College, Texas State Technical College–Harlingen, University of Houston, University of Houston–Downtown, University of Houston–Clear Lake, University of Texas at El Paso, Texas Southmost College, University of Texas–Pan American, and the University of Texas at San Antonio.

- Oversaw the development and implementation of Advice TX, in partnership with the University of Texas at Austin, by utilizing the College Access Challenge Grant to help establish a program that places recent college graduates as full-time "near-peer" advisors in high schools with low college-going rates. The program started out with fifteen advisors and now have 120 advisors in over 120 school districts in Texas. Institutions involved in overseeing the components of the program are Texas A&M University, the University of Texas at Austin, and two independent universities, Texas Christian University and Trinity University.

- Facilitated the development and implementation of Adult Basic Education Innovation Grants designed to establish pathways for adult education students who score below high school level but who have an interest in pursuing training at the postsecondary level. The following institutions have been involved in implementing these grant programs: Alamo College, Amarillo College, Austin Community College, Dallas Community College School District, El Paso Community College, Hill College, Houston Community College System, Lone Star College–Montgomery, San Jacinto College, South Texas College, and Tarrant County College.

- Oversaw the development and implementation of Mathematics, Science and Technology Teacher Preparation academies designed to improve the instructional skills of certified teachers and trained students in undergraduate and master's degree teacher preparation programs to perform at the highest level in mathematics, science, and technology. Institutions involved in the program included Stephen F. Austin University, Tarleton State University, Texas A&M International University, Texas A&M University–Commerce, Texas A&M University–Corpus Christi, Texas State University–San Marcos, the University of Texas at Arlington, the University of Texas at El Paso, the University of Texas–Pan American, and the University of Texas of the Permian Basin. More than five hundred teachers have received additional training and certification in the areas of math, science and technology.

- Managed the development and implementation of College and Career Readiness Initiative Faculty Collaborative to engage faculty members from

Texas Institutions of higher education associated with the delivery of educator preparation in becoming aware of and more familiar with state college and career readiness standards, The training focused and supported university–based instruction around mathematics, science, English language arts, and social studies. Four universities were involved in the development of the collaboratives: Texas State University focused on mathematics, the University of Texas at Austin focused on English language arts, Texas A&M University–Corpus Christi focused on science, and the University of Texas at Arlington focused on social studies. More than five hundred faculty members have been training in the implementation and delivery of the College and Career Readiness Standards.

www.ingramcontent.com/pod-product-compliance
Lightning Source LLC
Chambersburg PA
CBHW022050050726
47591CB00002B/479